CW00417667

GEN

Kickstart YOUR
Future

Thanks so much

Kerry

S.P. Walt

Simon Walter

Book Cover design by Charlie Walter
Photography by Sheila Burnett
www.sheilaburnett-headshots.com

CONTENTS

PROLOGUE

Springtime 2020. The world is gripped by an awful pandemic. COVID-19 is a killer virus which originated in China but has now migrated across the world and the UK is in lockdown. This is not a major Hollywood movie; this is really happening!

We are in unprecedented times. The streets are empty. Millions of people around the world are quarantining themselves in their own homes, coming out once a day for an hour's worth of exercise or to shop for essential supplies. A new term is coined, and social distancing becomes a constant concern. People queue to get in to supermarkets wearing gloves and masks to protect them from the virus.

All socializing and social events are cancelled. The world of sport has ground to a halt. Festivals and concerts are postponed or put on hold. World economies are in freefall. Only essential businesses are operating and where possible, people work from home. The less fortunate non-essential businesses have been put in to hibernation and their employees stood down.

Our National Health Service staff are going above and beyond the call of duty to save us and cope with this killer virus. Every Thursday evening people come out of their houses to clap and cheer for the key front line workers that are saving lives and keeping the country functioning.

There is a lot of concern for the elderly and those with underlying health conditions who seem to be more vulnerable to this virus. Communities are coming together to look after these people.

But there is one group of people who seem to have been forgotten or overlooked and this is a huge mistake.

Our young people.

Be under no false impression, never have our young people been so important. If you are one of these young people, never has the world needed you and future generations to come like it does right now.

Schools are closed and the upcoming GCSE and A Level exams were cancelled. This was a huge development for all of our young people. Formal education was suddenly interrupted and in some cases, terminated! The summer term 2020 is cancelled. Everybody stay home!

Although the exams are not taking place, each student who was due to take final GCSE or A Level exams in 2020 will be awarded a grade as if they had sat the exam. This grade will be based on previous mock examinations, effort and work carried out over the last two years and teacher's predicted grades. It has been said that these GCSE and A Level grades will be indistinguishable from previous years or years to come. That may be the case on paper, but how will they be viewed emotionally by the students who will receive them? Or the potential employers looking to hire them?

INTRODUCTION

When I first heard the news about schools closing and exams being cancelled it was quite emotional in our house. This development effects my family directly. My son Charlie, was due to take his final A Level exams and my daughter Alex, was due to sit her GCSE exams.

At first, there was some relief in our house when the news came out. The mock exams at the beginning of the year had gone well and the predicted grades were quite good. Initially, it seemed there may be an unexpected benefit in not having to stress out over exams and revision.

Soon the mood shifted from one of relief to one of sadness, disappointment and anger. Yes, for the grades and how they were being calculated but also for the way in which such a huge chapter of life was coming to an end. All the work that had been put in over the years in preparation for these final exams, seemed to be in vain when they were cancelled at the last minute. It was a shock to learn there were only two more days left of school. A further shock to discover there will be no "passing out parade", no leaver's party, no rite of passage from this chapter to the next. It seemed that the lights were being turned off on this era before students could emotionally prepare themselves to say goodbye to their childhood in the usual way.

When education and exams were cancelled, I reached out to young people affected by the COVID crisis and asked them to share their feelings and emotions. I was genuinely interested to see how young people felt and find out what they were thinking. Were my son and daughter experiencing the same reactions as their peers?

The responses I received were so powerful and so emotional that I found myself being moved by each and every one. I read and re-read each one over and over again. Each of them was raw and honest. I could tell that each one was a genuine first draft, and an instant outpouring of emotion. I asked my contributors for permission to share their thoughts and they agreed. I have added them as impact statements throughout this book for you to read first hand.

If you are one of the 2020 GCSE and A Level students missing out, then you will relate to these impact statements in some shape or form. If you are not one of the COVID-19 final exam disrupted students, I hope you will be able to learn from their experience.

IMPACT STATEMENT: AMY

Amy was due to sit her final A Level exams in Biology, Chemistry and History.

"From the moment I first started my A-Levels I knew that they would be one of the most challenging stages of my life. The work load was an unexpected step up from GCSE, considering I was only doing 3 subjects (Biology, Chemistry and History) compared to 10 subjects at GCSE.

The news that I received on 18th March 2020 regarding my A-Levels was a massive shock to myself and my fellow classmates. The cancellation of all A-Level and GCSE exams was always a fantasy to me and never would I have ever thought that this fantasy would become a reality in my life due to COVID-19. Initially, I wouldn't believe what I had heard on BBC News that evening, it just didn't seem real. My schools group chat on whatsapp, with the students from Year 13 were all as shocked as I was and there was confusion as we couldn't understand what we had just heard. I then started to celebrate the idea that I didn't have to sit my exams in May and June and at the time this seemed like a good thing. However, after much thought and processing of the situation, I came to a realisation that this was far from a good thing.

Throughout my A-Level journey, my mental health got to a state where I no longer wanted to be here anymore. Many young adults of my age go through this as we all have the stress and anxiety of doing well to set ourselves up for the future, and especially not disappointing parents.

I would say that Year 13 was the worst year for my mental health. In February 2020, I was officially diagnosed with Depression and I was put on Fluoxetine (an anti-depressant medication). Even though it was only recent that I was diagnosed with it, I had always known for a long time I suffered from it, just because of my actions and thoughts I was experiencing for months and even years beforehand. I have to admit, A-Levels weren't the only factor contributing to my depression, however it did cause other worries.

Some of these worries included money issues. Like many young adults, we all want new things and we all want to go and do things but as we know this all costs money. Now I certainly don't come from a well-off family so I had to go and get a job to be able to afford these things. This then had an impact of how much A-Level work I could be doing which consequently led to even more stress and anxiety.

Being told I wasn't going to have to sit exams was partly a relief for my mental health as I knew that the months leading up to my exams and during my exams would have been very dark for myself. However, it has brought the worry of what grades I will end up with. I wasn't one of those students that constantly got As or Bs in every single exam, I fluctuated a lot which is why I have a worry of what the outcome for me will be. My predictions are 3 B's but I was hoping to get at least one A which I had always set myself from the start of Year 12 and I knew I would have worked hard enough to achieve this.

The fact that everything is so uncertain as to whether or not I could potentially sit some exams is worrying for me and is partly disappointing as like many students, I put in a lot of time and effort to work and revise for my A-Levels.

One of the most disappointing parts of this whole situation is that the class of 2020 cannot celebrate the way they wanted. I will not be able to go to the pub after my final exam with all my classmates to congratulate everyone for getting through those horrible months. I will not be able to have a Year 13 leavers dinner that every other year has been able to have, or a prank day like in previous years. Our leavers day had to be planned in 2 days so it wasn't the one me and all my classmates were hoping for.

The whole situation is unimaginable however it has happened to me and the thousands of other Year 11 and Year 13 students and we will all be known as the Class of COVID-19. #covidkids"

Before we go on I would encourage all of you, whether your exams were cancelled or your education was interrupted, to talk about your own situation. Tell somebody how you feel or write down what you are going through. Just to share your experience, whatever that may be is a good way to keep you mentally healthy. All of the people who sent me an impact statement said they found the process therapeutic. It was a positive way to express their thoughts and let out what they really felt. It's also a great release to share. If you can't find somebody to read yours, send it to me!

I have a huge amount of sympathy for the way Amy is feeling. I remember when I finished my last A Level exams and school was done. It was over but in a way that made sense. There was a timetable leading up to that last day with a series of small and large milestones along the way that we could prepare for and celebrate. When that final last day came, we had closure on that two-year course and were able to bid a fond farewell to an institution we had spent 7 years in, together. Think about it. During the years you spend in education you probably see your school pals more than you see your parents, guardians or siblings!

Charlie, Alex and their peers right across the country have not had that closure. One minute they were heading off for school as normal and by the end of the day that was it. No warning. No time to really say goodbye. No time to process and reflect as they walked out of the school gates for the last time.

It was just gone.

A rite of passage has been stolen from all the final GCSE and A Level students this year, not to mention the millions of students across the globe. In addition to that, it was followed by many weeks in isolation to think about it and dwell on it. Don't. COVID-19 is not your fault. It's happened, let's deal with it.

CHAPTER 1 - WHY DID I WRITE THIS BOOK?

Before this COVID-19 pandemic arrived, the idea of a book for young people had been circulating in my head for a while. Why?

Why did I write this book? I could sum it up in one word really. Frustration! Frustration for young people. Not frustration with young people but frustration for young people.

Where did this book start? It all began just under a year before COVID-19. Slow down, I am not saying I can predict the future! My frustration was bubbling along but COVID-19 was the final straw! My frustration volcano erupted!

Let me explain.

It was late afternoon in the summer of 2019, long before anybody had heard of COVID-19. My son, Charlie, was driving me in to town. He needed to pick up a parcel from the post office. Charlie had not long passed his driving test so he asked if I would go with him. As we drove along and I pointed out all the driving mistakes he was making whilst holding on tight to the seat, our conversation turned to school. Charlie had just finished the first year of his A Levels. When he went back to school for his last year, the final exams would come around quickly, I told him. I asked if he was ready. Charlie told me he felt ready for the final year, but he wasn't so confident about what happens after the A Levels finished and he left school. In short, I sensed he was nervous.

Leaving the institution that is school, where everything is structured and organised and going out into the big wide world is a daunting prospect. I tried to reassure him with my experience of leaving school, getting a job and making my way in the world. Bottom line, there is a place in the world for everybody, but Charlie was still worried:

"I don't want to disappoint you and mum. I don't want to fail."

I asked Charlie what the number one worry he reckoned his school pals had at that moment in time. Charlie came back:

"Failing and disappointing their parents."

I tried to process this one in my head. Failure and disappointment at the tender age of 17? What amount of pressure were these kids putting on themselves? What amount of pressure were their parents, guardians and teachers putting on them? What amount of pressure was society placing on them? 17 years old and carrying the weight of the world on their shoulders!

At 17, I was more worried about having a girlfriend and trying to get into pubs!

That's when I realised that the pressure on young people today is immense compared to when I was finishing up at school. The world Charlie is about to step into is so much different to the world I stepped into almost 30 years ago. The pressure dial has been cranked up and this has been further compounded with COVID-19.

Mental health issues - especially in young people - are very much a hot topic these days. Why? Pressure! Society keeps jacking up the pressure. Pressure to succeed, pressure to fit in, pressure to be noticed, pressure to look right, pressure, pressure, pressure…

I believe we could eradicate a lot of mental health issues in young people if we dialed down the pressure. Unfortunately, society puts this pressure on us but there are a few tools we have that can help us manage that pressure. You all have them; you just need to access them.

So much emphasis is placed on success, but how do you define success? Getting on the property ladder? Having a flashy car to get you from A to B that will in all honesty, impress nobody; well not for more than a few minutes. Or is success happiness? Is success material or spiritual?

I used to think it was material. I had the nice cars, nice houses and lived a great lifestyle but a few years ago my mindset shifted. While those material possessions were nice to have, later in my career I realised that there was so much more to success. Success was happiness and I made a change.

I told Charlie that as long as he was happy, he could never disappoint me or his mum.

What's the key to happiness? You are! Be yourself.

I spent 25 years working for one of the biggest investment banks in Europe, running their foreign exchange and fixed income desks in some of the most challenging financial markets. I had the fortune of meeting people who inspired me and I also came across people who didn't. I experienced a rollercoaster of emotions as I climbed the corporate ladder with many highs and lows, but I came out the other side and I am happy.

As I reflected on my long career in the big wide world, I realised that I had picked up many tips along the way that could help Charlie. They might even help you too.

Your journey is just beginning and the most frequent question I hear from young people is:

"What am I going to do?"

The big question has a very simple answer:

"You are going to do…YOU!"

Stick with me and I will explain.

BACKGROUND

I was born in 1973. I grew up in Hertfordshire, just outside of London. My dad was a plumber and my mum was a librarian. I had one older sister, no pets and a very small box room.

My childhood was a relatively happy one. We were not rich, and we were not poor. My mum and dad gave us what they could afford growing up. We didn't go on foreign holidays; in fact, I didn't get on a plane until I was 19 years old! Prior to that I had only set foot outside of the UK once for a geography field trip to France and we had to drive all the way there in the school minibus!

I went to the local state secondary school which I enjoyed to an extent. I really went to school for sport. I was not great at any one sport, more of an all-rounder.

I wasn't super academic, so I had to work at school. Some kids seemed to get the top grades without even turning the page of a textbook. I put the effort in but I could have done more when it came to my GCSE's and A Levels. I coasted through education really.

In the final year of A Levels, the question of What do we do next? became slightly more urgent. The prospect of leaving education and going out into the big wide world scared a lot of us back then and scares even more young people today.

The institution of education is a structured and therefore relatively safe place to be. You know what to do and are told how to do it. There is a defined schedule and you arrive and leave at a certain time each day. You have a timetable of where you need to be and what you should be doing at any given point in the day. You know who you are going to see on a daily basis and roughly what you are going to be taught.

The very idea that you need to leave this comfortable environment and go out and make your own way is daunting for some. It's difficult to imagine leaving the safety of a well-defined daily structure for the unknown.

Some people can't wait to break out of these confines and are ready to strike out on their own with all of the freedom of choice that is sure to follow.

However, everybody is different. Some people know what they want to do and are ready to embrace the challenge, whilst others are paralysed by the abundance of choice.

In my experience, the majority of students don't really know what they want to do - and why should they? The average life expectancy in the UK is approximately 80 years old. At the point when you leave full time education you have only lived somewhere in the region of 20 to 25% of your life. How on earth could you have the next 75% of your life mapped out on the day you graduate from the institute of formal education?

I knew what I wanted to do to an extent. I would dearly have loved to be an actor but back then those opportunities didn't really exist. Drama classes at my school consisted of us standing around replicating the movement of a tree in the wind for an hour.

My school careers officer's advice was to "go and get a proper job, stop dreaming!"

My aspirations for a 'proper job' lay in the financial markets. I wanted to be a trader at a bank in the City of London. My dad was instrumental to this high-flying choice of career even though he did not realise it at the time. He often watched the business programme on the television and every now and again a report would come up about some big deal that was happening in the financial world. As the reporter gave us the story of the day, I was more focused on the backdrop of traders in the banks screaming and shouting at each other. It looked competitive and exciting. They all wore snappy suits, drove fast cars and looked like they were enjoying themselves. That was the job for me!

One day, in my Economics A Level class, our teacher Mr B, went around the room asking us all what we were going to do when we left school. The majority of the class wanted to go to University.

Around this time, University had become something that was a realistic choice for most kids coming out of A Level education. In previous years University was reserved for the rich kids or the super academic but in the few years prior to 1992 it became fashionable to go to University, and still is.

Back in 1992, University was also free. There were no tuition fees and tuition fees only came in to play in 1998. The problem was that by 1998, having a degree had become somewhat of a necessity in landing a job! How was the average student going to afford that much-coveted degree if it was no longer free? Hang on, student loans were available!

Get one…
Go study…
Go party…
Think about the debt later!

The theory was, if you had a degree you were guaranteed a high paying job, so students were encouraged not to worry about acquiring a student debt. Unfortunately, it didn't quite turn out that way for all students and many found that debt hung around their necks for a long time!

Twenty years later and society still thinks that way, even though half the degrees are not worth the paper they are written on. A degree doesn't give you a rite of passage for those high-flying jobs. I am not saying don't go to University. Just think about what you really want to do. And not what society expects of you.

We are only on page 20 and I have already gone off on a tangent! Back to Mr B and A Level Economics.

When it came to my turn to answer Mr B's question I replied that I would go and work in the city and become a financial trader for a big bank. Mr B nearly fell of his chair laughing. He told me I would never amount to much in the city and I should also go to University and get a degree.

When I was choosing my A Level subjects Mr B told me that I would be lucky to pass Economics at A Level because I had not done it at GCSE and I should look at a different subject. Basically, he had his favorites and I wasn't one of them. Bollocks to him. I was going to do Economics at A Level. Why should I compromise just because of him? His negative attitude made me even more determined to prove him wrong and I did! I managed to get a grade B in my economics A Level, quite a little bit better than the fail he predicted for me!

After leaving school with A Level's in Geography and Economics, I went on to have a 25-year career in finance working for one of the biggest Investment Banks in Europe. I started as the office junior and worked my way up through the ranks to Managing Director, running the Emerging Markets Foreign Exchange and Fixed Income trading desks. I spent 20 years in London and 5 years in Dubai where I sat on the board of the bank in the Middle East.

Teachers are supposed to inspire their students not kill their dreams, and if I'd listened to Mr B or let his opinions cloud my judgement or dissuade me from my goals, none of this would have happened. The lesson here is, if you want something bad enough, work hard for it. Even if others don't believe you have what it takes to do it.

Those 25 years were full of ups and downs, success and failure, laughter and sadness and many times I could have walked away from it, but I didn't. I met my wife in London and we have two wonderful children, Charlie my son and Alex, my daughter. I have travelled all over the world for the bank and met people from all backgrounds and cultures. I have met and worked with some wonderful people and I have met and worked with some complete arseholes too. As I said earlier, everybody is different! Through it all though I have stuck by my business ethics and it has rewarded me greatly. It has enabled me to walk away from the finance industry and pursue that dream job of acting that I yearned for all those years ago, but never pursued … until now. I will approach acting in the same way I approached finance. My method in finance worked, why not in acting? If you have a passion for something, and are prepared to work hard to achieve it, that is half the battle.

I believe that you can apply some very simple but valuable principles to whatever you want to do in in life, and see some truly wonderful results and release that pressure. I don't have a magic formula. What I am going to tell you is not rocket science. What I am going to tell you can be used by everybody in whatever you choose to do. I can guide you and teach you what I have picked up in my 25-year career but ultimately only you can determine your own destiny. Your life is a business and you are the product. What you do with that business and product will define you as a person and shape your tomorrow. Nobody cares more for your life than you do, so start caring how you live and start living like you care.

So, let's pick you up and dust off this COVID-19 and work out how you are going to be the best you can be irrespective of the level of interference this virus has had on your education. Let's investigate YOU!

CHAPTER 2 - CONDUCT A PERSONAL EVALUATION

Conduct a personal evaluation to determine why YOU want to start a business…

Too late! The business of YOU started when you were born!

Did you know that each company in the United Kingdom requires a 'Certificate of Incorporation' which is a legal document that shows you have formed and registered your company with Companies House? Your Certificate of Incorporation is your birth certificate! Companies House in this case is the world and you were 'registered' with the world when you were born.

Congratulations! YOU are a registered company and you didn't even know it! But what does your "registered company" aim to do? What is it going to achieve? How is it going to achieve?

CHAPTER 3 - CREATE A MISSION STATEMENT

Now that you've worked out you are a business, you need to find something for that business to do. Give your business a goal and a direction. Give your business something to achieve.

Firstly, YOU needs a Mission Statement!

What is a Mission Statement? A mission statement is 'a formal summary of the aims and values of a company, organisation or individual.'

It's a statement you make to aid you in achieving your goal. This will help guide your company and keep it on track. Your mission statement will change as you move through life. As you learn new skills, make new friends, encounter different people and life experiences you will evolve, and your mission statement will adapt accordingly. Some things that were once important to you might become irrelevant whilst other things will grow in importance.

Staying relevant in today's world is important because the world is constantly changing. We are now living in what is called The Fourth Industrial Revolution, a revolution that is guided by technological, digital and biological advances which bring both challenges and opportunities. The most successful people are the ones who adapt. They get a new piece of information and acclimatize to incorporate it. They don't sit there stubbornly sticking to the same plan with their eyes closed and their fingers crossed. No, they get off their arse and change direction. They stay relevant and therefore stay in the game.

I have had a few traders over the years who did not understand this concept. They would have a position in a currency or bond plodding along nicely. Then boom, a piece of news would hit the markets that didn't bode well for their position. Rather than sell that position and cut their losses they would sit there praying for the market to turn in their favour again. Of course, this very rarely happened and they got screwed. They lost a lot of money and a lot of respect. Nobody rated them, and as they say in the financial markets:

"You are only as good as your next deal."

Having the courage to change that position is what some traders lack. They don't want to admit they are wrong and they are fearful it will be seen as a mistake. That fear of making an error held them back and it could hold you back too.

Basically, the market does not care about the success you had yesterday, it only cares about the success you are going to have today, so don't screw it up. The markets have a short memory when it comes to the good things you do and a very long memory when it comes to your screw-ups! And the "market" is "life"!

Stay relevant! When things change, and unforeseen circumstances flip the script on its head, have the courage to make a change that keeps you in the game. Pivot and change with the times, rather than hoping it'll all turn out for the best.

When you are thinking about your mission statement ask yourself relevant questions.

Who am I?
What am I passionate about?
What can I offer?
Who will benefit?

Instagram's mission statement is:

"To capture and share the world's moments."

Your mission statement could be:

To help others.
To be successful in my chosen career.
To help others achieve their full potential.
To become the Pope!

To become the Pope? Really?

Back to my son, Charlie. In his final year of A Levels Charlie was asked by his teachers to be the subject mentor for Religious Education. He was tasked with helping younger students understand the subject better. He found this rather amusing seeing as he currently has no affinity to any religion. He was made subject mentor because he understood the subject well and what you had to do to achieve results in Religious Education. So, we joked with him that one day he could be the Pope! Obviously, his response was "don't be daft dad, there can only be one Pope at any time so it's a bit far-fetched!"

My point to him was not that he would become the Pope but that somebody has to do the job, so why couldn't it be him?

I would agree that the chances of him becoming the Pope are slim given he is not a devout Catholic, but he realised that the point I was making was relevant to life. Don't limit yourself! If you want to dream big, dream bigger! Set your mission statement, be it daily, weekly, monthly etc. to allow you to follow your dreams. Let your mission statement allow you to develop into your dream.

In Charlie's case his dream is to DJ at Ultra in front of 200,000 people. Again, my point to him is why not? Somebody has to do it! Dream big!

He took that message into his Music Production. He produces Electronic Dance Music (EDM) and is starting to see some success, getting his music out on to platforms and has even had one small label want to sign him up! All at the tender age of 18! So, Charlie is quite clear in his mission statement:

"To produce EDM music that people want to listen to (and DJ at Ultra!)"

This is what drives him on. He has a purpose and a goal through his mission statement which keeps him on track.

Recently Charlie was interviewed by a creative label to share his experiences and inspire other people.

The following is an extract from that interview:

"For some reason, there has always been this unwritten stigma around wanting to go and do something different or creative. Since I started making music over 2 years ago there have been many people who have been very negative towards what I want to achieve in life. Different teachers, friends and family have questioned my ability to make it in the music industry. I won't lie, this used to get me down all the time but in the end, I concluded that I was wasting my energy trying to express my passion to people whose opinions wouldn't budge.

So, I made a change. I started working harder on my passion than ever before because if I can't verbally persuade them to accept my choice then I am gonna show them. The momentum of my work has kept me going to this day because each day that someone makes fun of me or laughs at what I do, is another boost of energy to prove them wrong."

@diseekmusic | DJ & Music Producer

So, you can see, that Charlie, or Diseek as he is known in the music world has a clear focus. He has a clear mission statement which he lives by and has written on the glass doors of his wardrobe in marker pen! When he does get to DJ in front of 200,000 people at Ultra a new set of wardrobes is coming out of his first pay cheque!

At this stage in life you may not have a longer term mission statement like Charlie does, but that doesn't mean you can't have one.

You may have a daily mission statement, something you want to achieve on any given day.

Some of you know what you want to do in the future, some of you don't know yet. Define your mission statement by what is relevant to you today.

My mission statement for this book is:

"To help you realise you have all the tools you need to achieve your dreams and COVID-19 will not define you or your future."

Once you have your mission statement, make it public. Let people know what it is – and go out and do it. Share it with your friends and family. Give them a license to hold you to that mission statement and the power to support you in your journey. If you tell somebody you are going to do something you are more likely to go and do it.

Now we have to apply that mission statement to your company, so let's create a plan that's going to help you live it.

CHAPTER 4 - CREATE A BUSINESS PLAN

- What do I do?
- How do I do it?
- Who needs it?

What do I do?

You do YOU!

You have had lessons along the way. You have had influences and experiences which have defined you as a person. You have learned to communicate from being in the company of people who already knew how to communicate. For example, your parents or guardians. We have all seen the adult trying to teach the baby how to speak… "Come on, say Dada!" This is how you learnt. This is how you have developed. Some things can be learned by rote, like the alphabet or times tables. Others are innate, and these need to be nurtured and developed.

When you are young you have no fear. You learn what hurts and what doesn't by trial and error with some guidance along the way from others. Who you are develops as you grow through experience and learning. What defines you as a person? How you behave, how you interact with others. All of this comes from what you have learnt and will learn on your journey through life. In the business world, this is called professional development.

How do I do it?

'How' can I apply 'me' to my mission statement?

Let's say your mission statement is:

"To inspire others to achieve their full potential."

How do I do it? Do you have a story to tell? Do you have an experience that can benefit others? Are you a good communicator? Are you a good listener? This is all about the product. It's about you. Apply yourself to the mission statement. Your mission statement will have come about because of who you are and what you have become.

When I worked in the world of banking, one of my jobs was to explore new markets for the bank's customers to invest in. One of the biggest markets we discovered was Nigeria.

Up until that point, none of the western banks were providing investment opportunities in Foreign Exchange or Government Bonds in Nigeria. Local banks in Nigeria were doing it, but western clients were reluctant to place their money with the local banks as they saw them as a big risk. It was an unknown market and the local banks were not regulated like western banks were. The clients were not confident that if they put their money with the local banks they would get it back if the market went wrong. That was a common theme in some of the more challenging markets we operated in. Our job was to work out how we could put the client's fears to rest. We had to find a way for us to step in and bridge that trust gap.

We set out our mission statement before we did anything else:

"To be the number one provider of safe investment into Nigeria for western clients."

How on earth were we going to do that?

We were a big bank with a big name and that gave us leverage with the local banks. They all wanted to do business with us and were more than happy to sign all the regulatory agreements we needed to be able to facilitate business. We had to open bank accounts with the local banks and establish relationships with them. We had to introduce ourselves to this market.

Once our product was in place we had to sell it to our clients. They all wanted to be invested in Nigeria and here we were offering them a safe way to do it. Clients were happy to take our name on their deals as they all had existing and longstanding relationships with us. They trusted us. That's how we did it.

We - as a product - were developed, established, friendly and easy to work with. We went on to become the number one provider globally of investment into Nigeria. We had developed our product and built our reputation. People wanted to work with us and throughout it all we lived by our mission statement.

We made sure we delivered on our mission statement and that's the lesson. Don't promise something you can't deliver. If you are consistently delivering what you set out to do, people will want to work with you. The world will see your value and jump on it. If you are not delivering your mission statement at any given time, nobody will trust, or care for your product. Remember, YOU are the product.

Who needs it?

Who is your client base? Everybody has something that somebody else needs in the world. In Charlie's case, there are people out there who want music and Charlie can produce it. He knows his marketplace and who he is selling to.

In the case of Nigeria, we knew our market and who wanted our services. Know your market and who needs your product.

Are you looking to inspire others to achieve their full potential? Then identify who needs your inspiration. Can you see some people struggling where you believe you could add value? There is your target audience.

Whatever it is you have, ultimately you have something that other people can benefit from.... YOU. It doesn't have to be a specific skill or talent. There are many attributes you have that you don't realise other people want, such as time, energy and passion to name a few.

Remember Charlie's aspirations to be the Pope? Why was he made subject mentor for Religious Education? It wasn't for any religious affiliation. Charlie was made subject mentor because he demonstrated effort, good communication, positive attitude, strong work ethic and an ability to listen to other people's opinions and take them on board. Charlie had what the school needed (pupils = clients = market) to inspire others in the subject.

It sounds like I'm making Charlie out to be the Patron Saint of Product. Trust me, he isn't. He isn't the perfect rounded product, nobody is. He has his knock backs just like everybody else. Mistakes are life's way of telling you something did not work out quite right. How you deal with mistakes defines you as a person and adds another layer in the development of your product.

Charlie's mission statement and business plans will change as his journey continues. As you learn and grow, your goals will change and grow too.

This is why you constantly need to be 'developing' your product. What gets you through to the end of your education won't necessarily get you to the next destination on your journey. Your product is constantly evolving. YOU are constantly evolving. And if you don't, you will be left behind.

Some people plod through life never re-assessing their mission statement. They end up unhappy in their job, without any of the job satisfaction they might have had earlier on. You might even know somebody like this yourself. Somebody who really isn't happy but keeps doing the same thing, while failing to update their mission statement. I think we all know somebody who fits in to this category and it's a good lesson for all of us. If you don't want to end up bored, stagnant and unhappy then update your mission statement! Have the courage to stay relevant and re-assess your life choices from time to time. Change is hard, but sticking with an outdated mission statement won't enable you to achieve the happiness and success you seek.

Earlier, I said you were a company and so you are. Think of yourself as a 'start-up' in the world. You are just starting out on your entrepreneurial journey of developing and marketing your product!

CHAPTER 5 - SO, I AM A START-UP, WHAT'S THAT THEN?

A start-up is a young company, founded by one or more entrepreneurs in order to develop a unique product or service and bring it to market. By its nature, the typical start-up tends to be a shoestring operation, with initial funding from the founders or their families.

Does this tick the boxes for us? Let's break it down.

Young Company? Well you're young!

Entrepreneurs?

You are looking to make your way in the world, taking on the risk in exchange for reward.

Unique Product?

Every single person reading this is unique. I read the other day that the chances of you being born in the first place are 1 in 400 trillion! I won't go as deep as to explain the entire 1 in 400 trillion (purely because I got lost when it came to the figures regarding the actual biological reproduction process) but even if we just scratch the surface the chances of you being born are still quite remarkable.

In order for you to be born, your parents had to meet and in order for your parents to be born, their parents - your grandparents - had to meet and so on back through the generations.

My father was Scottish. He lived just outside of Glasgow. My mother was English. She lived in London. If my Grandfather on my dad's side had not had an argument with my dad when he was in his early 20's and kicked my dad out he would never have come down to London to make his fortune. Naturally it follows that he would never have met my mother and I would not be here today. If I wasn't here today then there would have been zero chance of meeting my wife, Alison. If Alison and I had not met, then my kids wouldn't exist. The chance meetings that have led me to the point where I'm writing this book are just mind boggling!

Just think about the odds.

There are approximately 7.7 billion people in the world today. The fact that your parents met and their parents and so on back through the generations is astounding. The fact that you have been given the chance of life is remarkable. Do not take that for granted. You have been given a gift, the gift of life. Use it!

Start living your life to its full potential! Dream big!

Market?

There is a market out there for what you have. Somebody somewhere is willing to pay for what you have. That could be a talent, an attribute, a skill to name but a few.

Shoestring operation?

Basically, an operation that starts with very little if that. Well, you started out with nothing when you were born, and you have got this far! You're good at this product development. You have already come a hell of a long way!

Initial funding from the founders or their families?

The founders or families are your parents/guardians. They feed you, clothe you, buy you the things you need to grow and develop. They have funded your product development so far and hopefully will continue to do so until such time as you are able to fund yourself!

So yes, you are a start-up. You're not an established business yet but you're working on that.

CHAPTER 6 - WHAT DOES A START-UP NEED?

A start-up needs a product. Ok, so we have that one covered. YOU are the product!

A start-up needs customers. Again, we have that one covered. We have already talked about a market for YOU. Somebody out there needs what you have.

You have the product and you have the customers. How do we let the customers know that there is a product they need? How do we let the customers know they need YOU? You need to market YOU.

The funny thing is, you have been marketing YOU since the day you were born, you just may not have realised it yet.

Everything you do is marketing YOU. The way you walk, the way you talk. The way you interact and behave with family, friends, colleagues and strangers. All those social media posts say something about you. When I was leaving school, there was no social media so our audience for marketing was a lot smaller. Now, you have an audience that literally spans the globe. If you post something on Facebook, Instagram, Tiktok or any other online platform you are being watched and people are forming an opinion of you. That can be a positive, but it can also be a negative.

We have all had a text message or an email that could be interpreted in a number of different ways. It is possible that a message you are trying to convey is misinterpreted by the reader with negative consequences. Your positive intention could be clouded or lost and opinions may be formed that are unjustified.

This might have happened to you already, or to someone you know.

Bottom line is this. You are in the public eye 24 hours a day, 7 days a week, so be careful about what you say. What you give out today can have consequences tomorrow. Stuff you do today could get you that big break in five years' time or it could cost you the deal! Here's an example.

A young student applied to a bank for a place in their graduate recruitment programme. The bank had been at their university actively seeking graduate recruits and the soon-to-be graduate student applied. This was the student's dream job, and on paper this student had precisely what the bank was looking for...

As part of the application process, the bank took a look at the student's social media posts. Everything looked normal. Skiing pictures, family photos, videos of cute cats falling off the sofa when they fell asleep. You know the kind of stuff I mean. But then, there was a photo from the previous year. The student was behind the wheel of a rather flash car raising a glass of champagne. The car wasn't moving and the student wasn't driving, but the image was open to interpretation. People could form the wrong impression that the student was, had been or was planning on drink driving. Definitely not the kind of image the bank was looking to be associated with.

Application: Rejected!

Massive overkill on the bank's part I feel but that's the way the world works. Reputation and perception is everything.

Moral of the story? By all means have social media accounts and profiles. The internet is probably the most valuable tool the world has today, and you need to be a part of it. Just be sensible and think ahead. Like the saying goes:

"Think before you speak."

I always used to say to my traders, if you're going to write an email feel free, but before you send it read it over again and then read it once more. Then check the list of people you are sending it to. Do they all need to be receiving this email? Is it relevant to all of them? What responses do you expect to receive? Are the people it's intended for going to understand your point? Basically, try and talk yourself out of sending it. If you can't talk yourself out of sending it then hit the send button.

However, let's not get bogged down with the negative sides of your marketing. The positive marketing opportunities available to you are endless.

CHAPTER 7 - 10 THINGS THAT REQUIRE ZERO TALENT OR MONEY

I came across a terrific image on LinkedIn several months ago. I replicated the message on the whiteboard in my kitchen for my kids to see and apply as they went into the final year of their GCSE's and A Levels. I hoped it would be motivating and put them in a positive frame of mind to tackle their revision and complete their GCSE and A Levels.

When it comes to school and exams, I have always taken the view that kids don't need any more pressure. Why would I pile more pressure on my kids when they have enough on their plates learning periodic tables and whether 'conscience' is a verb or a noun? Sometimes I think parents can overwhelm their children with meaningless moaning about revision and getting good grades. The way I see it, if you want to learn you will learn, if you don't you won't. No amount of ball aching from me is going to make my kids revise more! I know this is a slightly different approach to parenting, but I believe it's better to inspire young people to learn rather than dictate to them.

Anyway, back to my LinkedIn image and the whiteboard in the kitchen. Having copied the words on to the whiteboard I took a step back and realised this wasn't just for them. It was for everybody. I had been applying these principles to my financial career for the last 25 years. Throughout my career, I have met and worked with many people who possessed these qualities. In fact, when I think of the most successful people I know from the financial industry, they each embody these attributes and it didn't cost them any money or further education to do so.

These are the qualities and attributes that every start-up, every established business, everybody needs. Funny thing is, you have all of these tools at your disposal already, you just need to employ them.

10 things that require zero talent or money

1. Being on time
2. Work ethic
3. Effort
4. Body language
5. Energy
6. Attitude
7. Passion
8. Listening
9. Doing extra
10. Preparation

CHAPTER 8 - BEING ON TIME

Being late to anything is my pet hate. If I am late not only does it reflect on me in a bad way but it's also wasting someone else's time. It's just disrespectful. What gives me the right to waste somebody else's time? Thankfully my wife shares the same principle as me on this topic so I never have to wait for her to "get ready" before we are going out. She is always ready before me in fact!

Over 25 years in the financial markets I have had to interview many people for various jobs and my rule was always if a candidate was late (unless there were exceptional circumstance) I would not see them. I would send one of my juniors instead. If they could not be bothered to turn up on time for the interview who's to say they would turn up on time for work?

The financial markets never sleep. We had a clear time window when London would take over from Asia, so being late was not an option. We had clients to serve, orders to execute. We could not tell the guys in Asia we could not take over the orders because Trader X had overslept. It would be unprofessional.

Turning up early or on time creates a positive impression.

We employed Richard Robinson from the bank's graduate recruitment programme and he worked for me from 2008 until 2016. He turned out to be one of the greatest colleagues and friends I ever had the pleasure of working with. Richard had all of the items on our list of '10 things that require zero talent or money' and many more positive attributes to his credit.

However, Richard was not your average graduate intake. He had spent 10 years in the Army prior to joining the bank and had been a Captain in the Tank Regiment. Army training equips recruits with self-discipline and a number of admirable qualities, one of which is punctuality. Richard's regiment was one of the first to enter Basra in the second Gulf War and I guarantee punctuality was crucial to their mission. I knew in Richard we had quality number one ticked off and I could expect him to have a dedicated work ethic. The only time I ever saw Richard consistently late was when it was his turn to buy me a drink!

The average life expectancy in the UK is 80 years. Sounds like a long time, right?

80 years roughly equates to the following:
960 Months
4160 Weeks
29,200 Days
700,800 Hours
42,048,000 Minutes
2,522,880,000 Seconds

Let's just assume you are 18 now.

18 years roughly equates to the following:
216 Months
936 Weeks
6,570 Days
157,680 Hours
9,460,800 Minutes
567,648,000 Seconds

Whoa! When you look at it like that you've already used up a load of your time!

You currently have left:
744 Months
3,224 Weeks
22,630 Days

543,120 Hours
32,587,200 Minutes
1,955,232,000 Seconds

Oh and by the way, just reading these numbers saw your seconds go down by roughly another 56!

Obviously, the above is based on the average life expectancy in the UK at present so you need to know that the value of your "time" can go up as well as down. Besides, who knows how COVID-19 will impact our overall life expectancy in the years to come?

The point I am making is that time is the most important and precious commodity YOU have. Bottom line, you have no way of knowing how much of it you have. You have no idea how long it will last and when it does run out, it will run out very quickly. One thing you can never get back is time, so use it wisely.

My great friend and colleague Richard died in 2016 from a brain tumor. He was 40 years old. He was diagnosed with this brain tumor in 2015 and told he had one year to live. Nobody saw it coming. Here was a guy in the prime of his life. He had a wonderful wife, Charlotte and three young kids aged 6, 4 and 2. He had just run the Dubai marathon in 3 hours and 13 minutes, a new personal best from the countless marathons he had participated in. Richard was a fit guy. Life was good for Richard and then suddenly, it was all taken away!

The day Richard died I had the greatest revelation:

My time is not forever and I have no idea when it will run out.

This was the moment I made a conscious decision to get out of the financial world which had dictated my life for 25 years and do something different. Yes, it paid really great money, but I realized I hadn't been 'truly' happy for a while. I had spent 25 years in the industry at the expense of spending quality time with my wife and kids. Success should be measured in happiness, not money.

Why didn't I make this change earlier if I wasn't truly happy I hear you ask. Well the first thing to say is that for the majority of my 25 years in the finance industry, I was happy. I enjoyed my job and chosen career. I especially enjoyed my time in Dubai.

It was only in the last year or so that the enjoyment started to slip away. But I had a fear. A fear of what I would do with the rest of my life. I worried about what people would think of me giving up a very well rewarded job. I knew I had to make that leap of faith and turn my back on the financial world and all the material trappings that came with it, but I didn't have the courage. I had only ever known this one career since leaving school at age 18.

Losing Richard was the final straw. It was that lightbulb moment.

"I only have one life and I have no idea how long it will last".

I knew then that I had to make a change and his passing gave me the courage to act. It was time to do the things I wanted to do. It was time to watch my kids grow up. It was time to live the rest of my life.

Richard's death made me change the way I looked at life and that is a very sad thing to say. I hope you can learn from this without having to wait for such a crisis or tragedy in your own life in order to come to the same realization I did.

We are all ticking time bombs. The difference between Richard and the majority of us, is that Richard was told how much time he had left. We don't know that piece of information.

You only get one lap around the track of life, don't waste it. Do what makes you happy. Follow your dreams and live your precious life to the fullest. Don't let anybody hold you back from achieving. Don't waste your time and don't waste other people's time.

Don't be late, if anything be early.

IMPACT STATEMENT: BILLIE

Billie was due to sit her final GCSE exams in Triple Science, Math's, English Literature, English Language, Religious Studies, Design and Technology, History and Art.

"Initially, me and most of my friends were relieved. We were glad we didn't have to go through the painstaking revision anymore and the pressure to do well. To meet our parents' and teachers' expectations had been pushed aside.

But that was all momentary. We realised this meant we had lost the time to do so much better than we had done in the two rounds of mocks we had to push ourselves through. Not only that but half of us didn't even consider the possibility that the exams would ever be cancelled and so put little or no effort into them. We just needed to focus on the tasks at hand: getting used to the questions and exam conditions, realising where we went wrong and then trying to figure out how we could do better, and finally how to do it in our real exams. This only just clicked for me in these past mock exams. I finally knew what I had to do and how I could do better.

A couple of days after we finished the mock exams, they were cancelled - making all of our hard work and effort (or less effort and more understanding in some cases) all for nothing. Instead of the government doing something so we can get a fair score, they're using results that don't accurately compare us to other students or reflect everyone's abilities! This won't be so much of a problem for students who did the best they could and know that but for people like me who take time and wait for all of the puzzle pieces to fit into place before being able to do something with passion and to the best of my ability, this turn out is devastating. A friend of mine constantly says "this is why we need coursework in all subjects so we can still get an accurate grade" and now I have to agree - because she is right.

As you may be able to tell, the relief quickly turned into resentment and now frustration helplessness. Anxiety has quickly settled in place of relief. Nobody wants to see their hard work go up in smoke and now we don't have the chance to show what we can actually do we are suspended in a limbo of time - or anti-time - as these days now slip by with no goals, no happy memories of our final exam day, tweeting about how bad the questions were, complaining to the masses and the masses yelling "good effort" back. We haven't got leavers hoodies that everyone lives in for the exciting and relaxing period after we know we did our best in the exams. We haven't got the prom, which most girls dream of. As much as some hate to admit it, we dream of this day. What we would wear, who we would go with, the happy-go-lucky carefree attitude we would have, all of it!

This year that was all ripped away from us. It's like we have lost our right to move forward, but nobody wants to repeat this painful year again with people we don't know.

Again, we are stuck in a limbo of no time at all, waiting for results we didn't earn but are given, at the mercy of an inaccurate system that predicts what we would get from half-hearted scribbles in our books, past mistakes and teachers who may or may not think you deserve from prejudice, resentment or favouritism. Nothing about this is fair! I know this might sound whiny, but what else can we do?

This is where the anxiety appears. We now have no control over the future. We have no idea how we'll be marked or how well we will do and this effects the schools and subjects we go on to do. If at the start of the next term year elevens don't meet up to the same standard of the end of the previous year elevens, then we will be turned away from the schools we should've gotten into or told to change subjects because we didn't score high enough. We didn't know the gravity of all of this back then. Its stunted student's growth. We have no idea how this will affect our education or possibly job opportunities in the future; and that's scary.

Overall, we know nothing and fear everything. We are constantly picturing the worst-case scenarios. Disappointed with the success we won't reach because of the lack of preparation the government has for events like this, how to stop pandemics from spreading enough to cancel important moments in the lives of young people and how to deal with pandemics in a way that won't let others suffer.

All we can do now is hope this changes things for the future so nobody else has to go through this hollow feeling."

If Billie could do it all over again she would do things differently. Billie was not behaving in any way differently to most students who have been through the education system going back through time.

I was exactly the same as Billie when I was at school. The only exam that mattered was the final one, so I did not worry about the mocks and tests leading up to them. Everything would fall in to place when the real deal had to be done.

The problem is, the real deal has been cancelled and we can't turn the clock back and do things differently.

If I had made an announcement to every student back in September 2019, who was due to take final exams in Summer 2020 that said:

"In January 2020 a virus is going to come out of China which will spread across the globe in a pandemic that will kill many people and infect a great many more. The world will go in to lockdown.... Oh and by the way your final exams will be cancelled and you will be given a grade that reflects your work ethic, how much effort you have put in to the course, your attitude to learning and your teachers, not to mention how well you do in the mock exams. Just saying!"

...how many of you would have approached that final year in a different way? How many would have upped their game?

Granted, most people would have thought I was a complete nutcase but in the back of their minds would have been that niggling thought of:

What if Simon is right?

That niggling thought in the back of the mind might have been just enough...

You don't know what the future will bring so the lesson for ALL of us is to dedicate OUR best to everything WE do.

CHAPTER 9 - WORK ETHIC

The clients YOU are selling your product to will love to work with you if you demonstrate a good work ethic. What is a good work ethic?

Work Ethic: a belief in work as a moral good, a set of values centered on the importance of doing work and reflected especially in a desire or determination to work hard.

For me a good work ethic is a combination of 1 to 10 in our list above but with many more things thrown into the mix. Are you professional in what you do? Are you reliable? Do you get the job done? All of these attributes are a dream for the clients of YOU Limited.

In school, university, work or life, do you want to learn? Do you show a passion to listen to what your teachers are telling you? You do not have enough time in your life to learn everything you need to know from scratch. That's why you have teachers, mentors and people who can help you. It's a shortcut to the developed product. Remember, your teachers are helping you develop your product so show them a work ethic that befits your product.

I moved to Dubai in 2010. I was asked by the bank to set up a trading operation to cover the Middle East and Africa. I was given two options by the senior management. I could stay in London and build a team in Dubai that would report directly to me or I could move my family to Dubai and take a more hands-on approach.

In previous years, I had been on holiday to Dubai a few times. It was a nice place to go for a week or so but every time we got back on the plane to come home my wife Alison and I would look at each other and say "Lovely place for a holiday but I couldn't live there."

I came home from work that evening and told my wife the two options I had been given. Do it from London or move the family to Dubai.

Earlier, on the train home from the office as I worked out how I was going to present this choice to Alison I was pretty confident she would choose to stay in London. We had just finished renovating our house and Alison had overseen the whole project. There was no way she was going to leave after she had just finished it but I was so wrong! Alison did not even take the time to think about it or discuss it. She just said "Wow, now that will be an adventure," popped open a bottle of Champagne and proceeded to pack! That was it, we were off!

Building a trading operation in Dubai was not going to be easy. This was a big task. People to employ, systems to implement and so on. I wasn't going to be able to do this on my own and it became clear early on I would need a team to help me.

The first person I turned to was Richard. He had an MBA in Finance so he was well qualified to be in the industry. But it wasn't his MBA that made me want Richard in Dubai with me as my number two. It was his work ethic.

I would put a great deal of Richard's work ethic down to his Army days. As you know from an earlier example, Richard ticked every single category in our list above and many more multiple times over. I knew Richard would be an asset to my team, he was professional and reliable. He was the perfect fit to run and develop our business in the Middle East and Africa. Richard would go anywhere (well almost anywhere as you will find out later) and do anything to grow and manage our business. Richard had the work ethic I needed.

CHAPTER 10 – EFFORT

You have probably all heard of the saying "help me to help you." It's basically saying it's a two-way street. If you put the effort in, I can help you.

As I said, Richard wasn't your regular graduate intake for the bank. He had been in the Army for 10 years and when he came to my trading desk he didn't know how to trade. He didn't know the systems we used or the way we conducted our business. Why would he? Driving a tank did not require him to know how to buy and sell foreign exchange in the commercial markets, but from day one he was eager to learn. He didn't sit back and wait for us to show him how the markets worked, he did his own research and shadowed our traders. He was constantly asking questions and offering ideas and opinions.

This effort was noticed by the traders and they were keen to help him learn. It was clear from the outset this wasn't a guy they'd have to spoon feed. He was proactive and was going to learn fast. The traders knew that once he had the skillset required, it was likely their workload would become lighter allowing them to concentrate on their own markets. Richard quickly rose up the ranks of the bank because his efforts were noticed and we wanted to work with him. He quickly became a valued member of the team and we knew we had a great guy on board.

People notice effort and dedication. Richard and I were like chalk and cheese to an extent. I was straight out of secondary school, while he had the degrees. I was straight out of secondary school, while he had ten years' experience in the Army! I talked like a car salesman, he was a gentleman and an officer but we both had a common connection. We both had a heightened work ethic and realised we worked well together. We bounced off of each other. We matched each other's efforts and in our years together in Dubai this was very much noticed.

Effort is like a price tag. It demonstrates your value to your clients.

IMPACT STATEMENT: CHARLIE

Charlie was due to sit his final A Level exams in Sociology, Business Studies and Religious Studies.

"With the outbreak of Corona Virus bringing businesses, schools and society to a standstill I am left feeling troubled for emotions.

Being an "A-level Student" this entire fiasco to contain COVID-19 has in turn stopped schooling and ultimately cancelled my exams which I had been studying for the past 2 years.

As I said in my opening line I feel 'troubled for emotions' as part of me is glad I don't have to go through round 2 of stressing (ref GCSE exam period) whilst the other part feels cheated out of my 'sixth form experience.'

I feel it can be put best in the form of a football match analogy.

You get told that this coming Saturday there is the league cup final for your school football team. You get drafted into the first 11. From that point on you begin to practice and train whilst also worrying slightly about how well you'll be able to play on the day. Game day comes and you begin playing. As it approaches the closing stages of the match with the score level, you begin to feel confident in your abilities and everything is starting to slot into place. Though stressful, you can feel a goal coming from your team. But just as you get into your stride you're substituted and told to go home through no fault of your own. The stress of playing the final moments is gone as you know there is nothing you can do to change the outcome, however you are never told the final score until both teams can agree on what they 'think it should be' which defeats the rules entirely and creates this deep thought in the back of your conscious that worries what will be decided.

From this, I hope you can understand the roller coaster ride of emotions the government has taken all its young people on with us still not knowing conclusively how we will be examined.

From the announcement to cancel exams on Wednesday the 18th of March 2020 and to shut schools on the coming Friday, I think I speak for all A-level students when I say we experienced the most stressful, boring and strange mood within those 48 hours. I had never felt anything like it before and it is a mixture of feelings that are indescribable. You didn't know whether to work, play or try and make light of the situation.

I would never wish anyone to live through those 48 hours as we did. It was mentally draining and challenging with the intense unknown approaching.

It has now been exactly 2 weeks since that day and we are still none the wiser on how we will get results. Yes, there have been some rumors and exam boards coming out and making statements but personally I feel the government has been too quiet on this issue and I still believe that every student is experiencing the same levels of mental torture as if they were actually doing the exams. Haha! That was a nervous laugh by the way and one that comes with a strong headache due to worries about how my 2 YEARS of consistent effort will come down to people having a little chat.

Pros: I don't do the exams; therefore, more time can be spent on meaningful things i.e. music

Cons: You go through a mentally taxing experience whereby you're given no guidance or concrete statements and will be forever known as the year group that 'GoT LuCKy'"

Charlie is my son, so of all the students I asked to comment I know him the best and can analyse him fairly well! (Put your seatbelt on son, let's get started!)

"…my 2 YEARS of consistent effort will come down to people having a little chat."

Yes, it will. But aren't you glad that you put in the two years of consistent effort?

I think Charlie worked out the value of effort at the end of his GCSE's. Leading up to his mocks Charlie was exactly like me when I was at school. I would do just enough to get by and not get a stern talking to from my teachers and parents.

And just like me, Charlie's mock GCSE's were not exactly the greatest confidence builder going in to the final exams! Don't get me wrong, he didn't bomb but he wasn't exactly singing from the roof tops about them either.

After the mock results had come out and his mood was down he asked me if I was disappointed.

My response was as follows:

"Only you know how much effort you put in to these mock exams. You can tell me you put in maximum effort but only you know whether you did or not. If you are comfortable with the effort you put in that is fine by me, but only you can ever know that. Be true to yourself."

Later, Charlie came back. He told me that he had not really put much effort in and that he could have done a lot better. And I think here Charlie took away a valuable lesson:

Be true to yourself.

Nobody cares more about your life than you do so start caring how you live and start living like you care.

As it turns out, Charlie's final GCSE results were a massive improvement on his mocks.

After the GCSE results came out Charlie asked me if I was proud of him?!? Of course I was proud of him! Let's just say he got higher grades in all his GCSE's than I did!

Given the events of COVID-19 I am glad Charlie took that effort lesson in to his A Levels. I am also sure he will never let me forget that both his GCSE and A Level results are better than mine. I am still a better driver than him though!

Bottom line, you never know when an outcome in your life will come down to "people having a little chat". In the corporate world I come from, promotions, bonuses, hiring and firing all come down to "people having a little chat" and the content of that little chat is directly determined by the effort you are putting in. The ones who reap the rewards from people having little chats are the ones that consistently put the effort in. So don't just put the effort in when you think somebody is watching or when you want something.

Somebody is always watching.

This is how the real world works. You put in the effort and then people have a little chat. You may never even know they had a chat about you, but that little chat they did have, unknown to you, could have consequences for you in the future.

CHAPTER 11 - BODY LANGUAGE

Body Language is a huge part of our communication skillset. It is said that body language is 60% to 65% of your communication. How you 'hold' yourself makes a statement without you even speaking.

Having finished my A Levels, I was fortunate enough to get a job in a city bank quite quickly after I left school. It didn't just fall into my lap though, I had to put the effort in to get that job.

I went to the library (the internet wasn't available then, let alone Google!) and researched all the merchant banks I could find in London and wrote a letter to each of them asking for a job. Of the 20 or so financial institutions I wrote to, all but two came back with "Thanks but no thanks".

To start with, this was really hard to take. It seemed nobody wanted to hire me as I didn't have what they needed. I was demoralised. Perhaps this was not the job for me, and the replies were telling me that. I could have taken the defeatist attitude believing Mr B was right. But I didn't.

I was on the verge of giving up when my dad sat me down after yet another rejection letter had come in the post. He told me that somebody out there wanted what I had to offer, I just had to find them. The following day the final two letters arrived and both wanted me to go for an interview. Wow!

I thought the first interview went well but I was wrong. This was the first time I had been to a formal interview and I think I came across a bit nervous. The letter came through a few days later thanking me for attending the interview but I wasn't what they were looking for at that time. Fair enough, I thought, with my Dad's wise words echoing in my head. Somebody out there wants me; I just have to find them.

When I went to the next interview, I was more relaxed. I was more confident. I had prepared myself better for the interview process. I knew a little bit about the bank and what they did from reading what I could in the library and demonstrated that knowledge to the interviewer. The experience of the previous interview had been worth it and I immediately clicked with the guy interviewing me. As a result, my body language was more positive. I sat up straight and made eye contact. There wasn't a gap in the conversation. No nervous, awkward silences and I made sure to ask lots of questions which I had prepared in the days leading up to the interview.

I was really pleased with how the interview went and I got the job! I started working for the London branch of a small American bank in their back office and my job was to process all the foreign exchange deals that the traders in the dealing room were executing. I really wanted to be one of the traders executing the deals, but it was a starting point. I was able to interact with the traders every day and start building relationships. I had my foot in the door. I just had to be patient, work hard, persevere and wait for the right opportunity. I was in the right place to get noticed!

After I had been in the back office for about three months the junior trader in the dealing room left. He was off to a bigger bank having learnt the ropes at this small American Bank. The role of Junior Trader was now advertised internally in the bank and I jumped at the chance and applied. There were four of us who applied. The other three had been working for the bank a lot longer than I had, so I believed I was the outside shot, but that wasn't going to stop me. At the very least it was going to be a good experience and add to my learning curve.

Part of the application process was an interview with the big boss of the dealing room in his office on the 2nd floor. I had never even spoken to him before. I used to come in and out of the dealing room all the time collecting the deal tickets, but the boss had no idea what my name was. To him I was just the back-office boy. The thought of having a one-on-one meeting with him in his office whilst begging him for the opportunity to prove myself in the dealing room was rather daunting, but one of the senior dealers I had come to know really well gave me some advice.

He said:

"When you go in, be confident and make a connection. Stand up straight but relax. You need to look like you deserve to be there, that you don't look out of place. Shake a confident hand and make eye contact. Don't stare, but keep an active eye contact. If you constantly look away, you will look nervous and awkward. In short, make him notice who you are and what you want."

I thought to myself:

"Wow. I have to do all of this AND talk?"

The day of the interview came and I knocked on the office door. Upon hearing the word "Come," I entered confidently and stood in front of the big boss's desk. He had his feet up on the desk, relaxing, reading some papers. After what felt like an age he lowered his papers and I stepped forward to shake his hand. This made him have to take his feet off the desk and lean forward to shake my hand. As I shook his hand, I looked him straight in the eye, smiled and introduced myself. He smiled back. For the rest of the interview he didn't lean back once as we had both made a connection which grew stronger as we talked.

I got the job and not long after I started in the dealing room I asked him why he had picked me instead of the other three who had been in the bank longer than me.

He replied

"You had the job before you even opened your mouth! I spotted confidence and hunger and I like confident hungry people in my dealing room."

So it's true! Your body language can send out messages and you're in control of what those messages communicate.

Try this exercise that I was introduced to in one of my early acting workshops. It might be a little difficult with social distancing requirements, but just do the best you can. Find a partner and sit in front of each other quite close, within touching distance. Now for the next five minutes just look into each other's eyes. No talking. You will naturally react to what you are seeing or feeling, and your partner will do the same.

At the end of the five minutes tell each other what you could 'see' in each other's faces… perhaps you saw sadness, happiness, confusion, joy, anger. You will be surprised at just how spot on you were with your observations. The point of this exercise in the workshop is that acting is not just about saying some lines. Your facial expressions and especially your eyes can tell a story without you even uttering a word.

Body language is a very powerful tool. You have it and guess what? It's free.

CHAPTER 12 – ENERGY

Energy comes in many forms. Physical and mental to name a couple.

As you've heard, I spent five years living and working in Dubai. If you have been to Dubai, you will know that the climate is quite pleasant for most of the year. It's like having a very good English summer all the time but for a few months of the year the temperature hits 50 degrees celsius in the shade and the humidity goes through the roof. You can walk from the front door to the car and end up looking like you just got out of a swimming pool fully clothed!

Extreme heat like this can make you lethargic and tired and it can be tough to motivate yourself. In my first year in Dubai, when it came around to the really hot months I struggled to do anything. I felt drained and had zero energy. A work colleague gave me some wonderful advice. He said: "Energy begets energy".

For a moment, I wondered if he was trying to solve my problem with a little bit of Shakespeare and I really had no idea where he was going with this, but thankfully he went on to explain. He told me that if I wanted to feel more energised I should go to the gym and work out. Yeah right! What is this clown talking about? I'm already feeling bloody knackered and you want me to go do 10km on the treadmill and lift half a tonne of weights? And this is meant to make me feel energised?

He simply replied

"Yes".

I took his advice and went to the gym after work that night and funnily enough, at the end of the workout I did feel fresh, and I did feel alert. What's more, when I woke up the next morning I felt a bit of a spring in my step. And that is how I learnt to deal with the extreme heat of Dubai!

You have to look after your body as well as your mind. The body is a very resilient tool and left to its own devices it will function ok. Most people go through life without specifically exercising their bodies and they go on just fine but even a little bit of exercise can have a significant and positive impact on your general well-being. So, don't forget to exercise your body as well as your mind.

Energy begets energy or in the Queen's English "Energy will attract energy". If you engage in life with a positive energy you maximise your potential. People will notice your energy and reciprocate it! Energy is infectious!

The most infectiously energetic person I have ever met is a guy called Chris Ballard. Chris has so much positive energy, nothing phases him. Nothing is impossible for Chris. The world could be falling apart right in front of him, but Chris would still have a smile on his face and be ready to make you laugh. Let me tell you how I met Chris.

Just before I got married in 2000, I was asked to build up our trading operation in the Emerging Markets Fixed Income market. We would buy and sell Government Bonds from different countries in the emerging market world. Our biggest markets were Russia and Turkey. We had a desk doing it, but we were ranked number 10 in the league table of banks offering this service. This was not good enough for a bank of our size. My boss wanted to be number one and because I had a track record of building businesses for the bank I was asked to go and get our name up the league table in the client surveys.

We had to somehow get more clients coming to us to do their deals rather than going to our competitors. When I got on the desk I quickly realised that the problem was we were not offering the clients enough liquidity. The one complaint that kept coming up time and time again from our sales guys was that we were not giving the clients enough liquidity. In short, if our clients wanted to do big deals we were not accommodating them. If a client said I want to buy 100 million dollars (USD) worth of Russian bonds, we were only offering them 25 million USD worth and then asking them to leave us with an order to fill the other 75 million USD. This was not good enough for our clients. Our competitors were not offering the full 100 million USD but they were offering more than the 25 million USD we were willing to quote for.

It was clear we needed to change this. If we couldn't at least match what our competitors were offering, we weren't going to rise up the league tables as voted for by the clients.

The problem was, we could not hold that risk on our books. If the clients bought bonds from us, we had to go into the market and buy them. We could not deliver the bonds to our clients if we didn't have them. It's a bit like me selling you a chicken I don't have. If you pay me for a chicken I need to give you a chicken. If I don't have one, I need to go find one and buy it so I can give it to you.

If a client takes 100 million USD worth of bonds from me that I haven't got, I need to go find them and buy them. But that's a big amount. The standard size transaction between banks looking to cover their client's positions was 5 to 10 million USD at a time. That would mean to buy the 100 million I had just sold to my client I would have to find between 10 and 20 other banks that would be willing to sell me their bonds. Not an easy task when everybody knows you want to buy. The other banks are not going to sell me their bonds if they know I need to buy a lot more and the price is going to go higher. They will keep theirs and sell them for the higher price when the market has moved up. and if I can't buy the bonds at a cheaper price or at worst the same price at which I sold them to the client then I am going to lose money.

Losing money is not an option. Traders that lose money don't last long funnily enough. I needed to identify somebody that could find me the 10 to 20 other traders in the market and buy the bonds for me at the cheapest possible price.

Two days before I was due to get married I got a phone call from a broker called Chris Ballard. He worked for a broking company.

Brokers were the main source of liquidity for us. They were the guys that in theory could find us the 10 or 20 other banks that would sell us the bonds. They were independent companies from the bank. Broking companies made their money by charging us a commission on all the trades we did with them. I already had four brokers who weren't able to get me the number of bonds I required so why would Chris be any different?

I entertained the call and explained I was going off to get married and would not be back for three weeks as I was going to Australia for my honeymoon. I didn't expect much of Chris so I kind of went through the motions on the phone call. I outlined what I needed, and Chris promised me that by the time I got back from Australia he would have a plan in place to find me the liquidity I needed. Yeah sure, I thought and went off to get married not holding out much hope for Chris and his plan.

The day I got back from Australia, Chris called me again telling me he was the man to solve my problems. I admired his energy and persistence. I hadn't exactly warmed to his telephone call the first time around and I wasn't showing him much interest on this call either, but Chris was not giving up.

A few days later I sat down with my boss and explained to him we were going to have to offer a better service to our clients than our competitors. We would have to match their expectations for the size of the deal they wanted to do and see what happened. I explained we could lose money as we were not guaranteed to find the size the client wanted and the price could move against us but we had to give it a go.

When I got back to the desk I got another call from Chris. He said he had the contacts and liquidity I needed. At this point I had nothing to lose and decided to give Chris a chance. The other brokers were not getting me what I needed so I might as well give Chris a shot! We agreed the commission I would pay him for every trade he executed for us and we advertised to our clients that we were in the market to match anything they wanted.

Later that week a client called asking for a big amount. It was time to honour their request and put Chris's plans to the test. We traded with the client and I immediately called Chris telling him what I needed. "Leave it with me" he said. I put the phone down and prayed. Was I about to get completely screwed on this trade?

Five minutes later Chris called me back. He had all the bonds I needed and he had secured them at a better price than I had sold to the client. I was surprised to say the least. Was this beginner's luck?

Over the next week or so Chris did not let us down once and he quickly became my number one broker. Here was a guy who put himself out into the market and left no stone unturned when it came to fulfilling my needs.

This was the start of a wonderful relationship.

Chris is the kind of person that would do anything for anybody. Chris would walk that extra mile for you if you needed him. There was no bullshit with Chris. If he said he was going to do something, he did it. His attitude, work ethic and passion made all the difference, but his energy was infectious.

Chris knew how to sell himself. He realised very early on that what you as his client bought into was not the company he worked for. We were not buying in to the broking house. Chris learnt that what his clients bought into was him and as a result he presented himself as 'the product.' Chris could have been working for any company and it would not have made a difference because what we invested in was Chris, not the institution he worked for.

Chris lived and breathed 'product Chris' and still does. Chris was not some University educated genius. Chris was an Essex boy who could have been just as comfortable and successful selling fruit and veg on a market stall as he was in a broking house. Chris believed in himself and backed himself. Chris was - and still is - a product and you can't not buy in to him or his energy!

In our first year of trading we went from number 10 to number two in the league tables. In the second year, we went to number one and we stayed there for the next six years until I moved on to build a new business in the Middle East. Our competitors could not work out how we were doing it. We were doing it because of the solid relationship we had with Chris.

Chris wasn't just a broker, he was an all round nice guy. He took an interest in my family and I took an interest in his family. Chris knew the value of relationships, building trust and working as a team.

Chris' daughter Emily works in the city now, also as a broker. Whenever I see Emily, she tells me how the market still talks about Chris and me.

"You are both legends in the market still and nobody has replicated that success to this day. When I tell people my name, they ask me if I am Chris Ballard's daughter and do I know Simon Walter? When I say yes, Chris is my dad and Simon is like my stepdad they are impressed."

I have known Chris and his family for 20 years now and he remains my best friend to this day.

IMPACT STATEMENT: MAX

Max was due to sit his final A level exams in Art, Biology and Sociology.

"When I first heard about the A-levels being cancelled, I was sitting with a friend in my bedroom and we'd got a phone call from his sister. She was watching the news (very responsible unlike us) and was dictating what the government were announcing. As soon as the words were mentioned that we would no longer have to take exams, we just started screaming with excitement! We called practically everyone in our year groups from our phone contacts, screaming down the phone for a solid 10 minutes. However, something was bothering me and I didn't quite understand what it was. I didn't realise what it was that was bothering me until few weeks later, after the news set in.

Now that I've had some weeks to think about what happened, I actually feel almost cheated. The two years plus I had spent building up to this very moment almost seemed like a waste of time. All the effort I had committed to this aspect of my life had been ripped away. Even though I understand that the entire world is suffering and everyone in my age group across the globe is going through the same thing, I still feel as if a huge part of my life has disappeared.

I think I feel this way mainly because of all the expectations and pressure that is put on me as a student, especially one in a "private" school. Now whilst I realise that I am unfathomably lucky to be going to a fee-paying school, which I feel has eliminated a large proportion of negative aspects of school life, I feel that this side of the education system has a glaringly obvious fault that no one seems to pick up on. That being school performance. Across the globe the pressure from the school that they put on the teachers to make the best of the best students in such a results driven world. Ultimately this pressure is transferred directly on to the students.

So the past few weeks have been particularly hard for everyone, including myself. School for me, whilst being a place I despised for a large proportion of my life, seemed to evolve into a hub of community and friends these past few years. When the announcement of schools closing occurred, I didn't believe it. I then proceeded to go into school for the last day of my life, without time for mental preparation. I still didn't believe what was happening.

This last day however was one of the most memorable. All of the teachers became friends, all of our peers became emotional wrecks (a side I have never seen of the 'hard nuts' before!) and we had genuine fun. We had a brilliant idea of making a cardboard cutout of our favorite art teacher, dressing him in his traditional paint splattered lab coat and poking him through classroom windows and ultimately getting a selfie with our headmaster himself!

So, for me, about losing a rite of passage on the last day of school, I feel that we still got form of this rite and made the best out of an awful situation.

After all our best friends coming together on that last day and being our beautiful selves, making the day not a gloomy and miserable one, but one of the best yet….well then the seriousness of the situation set in. COVID-19 was a pandemic at large, and people were being warned of a potential lockdown.

New worries set in. My mum for one has had an autoimmune disease for the past 9 years of her life, and is especially vulnerable in this situation. For this I'm worried for her life, which is an emotion I have never experienced in my life. So many people have hidden problems of their own, like mine. Our lives for one are going to be changed indefinitely.

With regards to my future I am looking for a career in the creative arts industry. I feel that my future is probably one of the most unaffected and predictable (as predictable as being an artist can be). My foundation course is keeping me updated with regular updates which is reassuring, and they are predicting classes to hopefully commence as usual in September. But nothing is absolute. As for my friends, I feel that we're all in similar situations, with some looking for futures in the army, and others in a creative industry. However, I've got to be honest with you Simon, I'm shitting myself with regards to my future. But this is probably a fairly standard response when A levels are over, prematurely or not.

In a sort of summary, I feel that this whole episode of our lives will do one of two things, as black and white as that sounds. Everyone has a choice in this situation, to be sluggish and demotivated, or to get up off your arse and do something productive and grow as a human. All these experiences will no doubt shape my life as well as others, and I'm making it my responsibility to ensure my life is shaped to how I envision it. This means keeping on top of my mental state, keeping active indoors and finding things to do. So I'm going to continue to learn through the online courses my school is offering, work on my project bike, exercise and keep in contact with my amazing friends."

And there is the energy and determination.

I love it!

"Everyone has a choice in this situation, to be sluggish and demotivated, or to get up off your arse and do something productive and grow as a human……..I'm making it my responsibility to ensure my life is shaped to how I envision it."

There is the mental energy and determination Max is engaging in to turn this situation around and get on top of it, engaging his mind and body with activity. He is determined that COVID-19 will not shape his life.

CHAPTER 13 – ATTITUDE

Nelson Mandela once said:

"Do not judge me by my successes, judge me by how many times I fell down and got back up again."

If you have not read the story of Nelson Mandela I would encourage you to do so.

Nelson Mandela was a South African freedom fighter. He spent 27 years in prison for his political views, fighting for democracy and equality for all. Upon his release from prison, Nelson Mandela went on to become South Africa's first black President, ending white minority rule and promoting democracy and equality for all. His attitude to life has been a great inspiration for many all over the world.

Life is not easy; you have to work at it. Some things come naturally but most things, well you have to work for them. You will experience highs and lows and you will taste success and failure. How you deal with it is key.

I have had many experiences like this over my career in finance. Many times, I could have just crawled away and hid but I learned a very valuable lesson early on in my trading career.

In one example, I had been given the responsibility of one of the major trading books in the bank while the senior trader was away on holiday. I started off making good money, trading the markets in small sizes and my confidence grew. I started trading bigger sizes, thinking I had this market licked. Just when I thought I was the king of trading, the market collapsed on a piece of news that was unexpected and I had completely the wrong position. I owned the wrong currency when the market was collapsing! I lost all of the money I had made and then some more on top! I was mortified. My boss had given me this opportunity and I had blown it. I had been too sure of myself, too cocky! The boss came to me and I braced myself for an absolute bollocking.

Surprisingly, the bollocking never came.

He sat me down and said the following:

"Learn from this experience. Realise what you did wrong. You lost money, embrace it. Learn to lose and you will appreciate winning so much more."

To this day, I have never forgotten that valuable lesson. Every trader I have ever employed has heard this lesson from me too. I think this is possibly the most important thing I have ever learnt in my life.

I picked myself up from that incident and went on to make all the money I had lost back before the senior trader returned from his holiday!

Your attitude to life defines you. I didn't just sit and moan about my loss. I had fallen down, but I got back up again and that is what I was judged on.

Your attitude has the ability to make you stand out, to let people know your value to them. We love positive attitudes in our lives. They inspire us and lift us and a positive attitude rubs off on others. When I was in the financial world, I would always aim to build a team around me full of positive attitudes. It got results time and time again so why change it? That was part of my business model and I stuck to it.

When I turned up in Dubai to build a trading desk for the bank there was already a small team in place. Whenever I was asked to go in and fix something for the bank, I would always spend time watching and listening when I got there. I couldn't just walk in and make a snap decision. I wanted to give myself time to evaluate the situation and come to the correct conclusion.

In Dubai, some things were working well but it became apparent very quickly that the attitude of the office was not quite right. It was quite negative. People were sitting back and waiting for something good to happen and of course, nothing good was happening! They were waiting for big deals to come to them but the problem was nobody knew they were there waiting and so nobody brought them the big deals they craved. They assumed that because they worked for a big bank with an established reputation in the financial markets, business would just naturally flow their way. They believed the markets owed them a living because of who they were and where they worked. Unfortunately it just doesn't work that way. The world does not owe you a living just because you showed up. You need to go out and earn it.

I had to make some changes and quick smart! I needed a structure that would complement Richard and myself. For the past two years, we had been on a rollercoaster ride for the bank generating a lot of success so I knew we could do it again here. It was a tried and tested model. Richard, taking his experience from the Army would say "we don't need officers, we need soldiers." We had the officer. Me. We had the Sergeant, Richard. What we also had in that team when we walked in was one other Sergeant and one Private. The Private was young, hungry and eager to work. The Sergeant was a little battle weary. They could not see anything positive. Everything was negative in their eyes with no clear way out.

The first thing we did was to hire a new graduate for the desk. We needed someone fresh and enthusiastic in the team. We went through the recruitment process and settled on a young woman by the name of Nadine Hagar.

Nadine came from Egypt and had graduated from the University of Cairo. The banks' Human Resources department and some of my senior colleagues were over the moon. They ran around telling anybody who would listen that Nadine was the first female graduate from a Middle Eastern university ever to be hired by the bank. Personally, I found that a bit annoying. I did not want Nadine or our team to be tagged with the 'hired for political correctness' reasons. We had not hired Nadine to tick a PC box or to make the statistics for the bank look more diverse. Nadine was hired on merit, not because she was female and from Egypt. For us, Nadine had been hired because she demonstrated all the attributes we were seeking, but what I loved most about Nadine was her attitude.

Nadine was a positive person and her attitude demonstrated this. From day one Nadine wanted to learn everything we knew, and this is where Richard came in to his own. He was a great teacher. However, there were times when Nadine got frustrated and low. Everybody has a 'bad day at the office' but it's how you deal with those bad days that speak volumes.

Around a year or so after joining our team, Nadine had a huge mistake dumped on her from a rather large height. An error from the sales department had left us with a lot of money trapped in a market that was extremely difficult to get out of, if not impossible. We were potentially staring down the barrel of a big loss. When I say a big loss, I am talking about millions of dollars. Ten million dollars in this case! The sales guys had called up to deal with Nadine on behalf of their client but had executed the wrong trade. That left Nadine 'holding the baby' so to speak. Even though it was not Nadine's mistake, she ended up having the problem reflected in her trading book. The sales guys did not have a trading book or a profit and loss account so we had to wear it and Nadine was quite upset about it, to say the least! Something that was out of her control was currently showing up in her trading book as a potential ten million-dollar loss! She stomped around for the rest of the day. She was understandably angry and frustrated. By the following morning though the old Nadine was back and she had a plan.

It took around six months to get all of the money back out, but Nadine didn't rest until she got every last dollar. Her attitude was first class. Day in, day out, she would be calling everybody and anybody asking if they had some business we could do in that market that would help us get our money out. Slowly she found clients that had the opposite trading interest to us and this enabled her to get our money out, bit by bit.

The day the final dollar came out Richard and I both sat back and agreed, "now THAT is why we hired her!" Other traders I have known would have just crawled under a rock and tried to forget, but not Nadine. Nadine was determined to get all the money back and prove to us that she had what it took to succeed: the right attitude. Nadine took somebody else's problem, repackaged it with her attitude and spat it back out, solved!

Nadine still works in the financial markets although not for the same bank anymore. Her reputation in the Middle Eastern markets is first class. If anybody wants to know anything about those markets Nadine is number one on their speed dial. Nadine's attitude leads to bigger and better opportunities all the time and I've enjoyed watching her succeed and build her career over the years.

Remember, attitude is a price tag. It is a price tag that advertises the value you can bring to YOUR clients.

IMPACT STATEMENT: ANNALISE

Annalise was due to sit her final GCSE exams in Triple Science, Maths, English Literature, English Language, Spanish, Music, Religious Studies and History.

"On the Wednesday that they were cancelled, my mum had just picked me up from my Spanish speaking practice after school. We were listening to the radio as we were coming home and it was announced that school was closing on Friday. Then when we got indoors we put the news on and it announced that exams were cancelled. I was very upset and cried a lot that evening as I worried for my future. Will I ever be able to go to a good university if I have no GCSEs to prove myself? Will I still be able to study medicine? Is my future going to be severely affected due to the exams being cancelled?

The next day at school (the Thursday) I cried a lot as well (I know right, what a loser I am crying in front of my friends ha-ha). The Friday was my last day of school and it felt so surreal. It didn't feel like I had time to say goodbye to my school friends and my teachers. That was it. I was leaving. After that day, I would never go back into that building and see the majority of those people again. It felt as if I was having to deal with leaving even though it hadn't sunken in yet.

I was also very upset as I had worked so hard all throughout high school (especially the last two years). I was never a student who messed around, I always did my homework and then extra. I stayed after school numerous times a week to have private tutoring to push my ability further. I had pretty much finished making all of my revision notes and cards, only to suddenly find out that all my work was pointless. I felt as if all of my years at school had been building up to this moment: the moment when I could walk away with amazing grades to take me on to further education and be successful in life. When I was in primary school I was bullied by the other pupils in my class throughout most of my primary school experience. I remember always thinking that one day I would be more successful than them and they'd wish they were me one day.

However, by the time I'd gotten to high school, I didn't want to succeed in life and get great grades to prove my previous bullies wrong in life any more. I wanted to do it for me.

For a while now I've wanted to work in healthcare. A couple of years ago I decided I wanted to be a dermatologist and I still hope to fulfill this aspiration one day.

I guess you could say all in all that I wanted to take my GCSEs to prove to myself and future employers that I can put in the hard work and get great results; after all, you reap what you sow.

Although I am still very disappointed and anxious as to what will happen with the exams this year, I still have a positive outlook on the future as I am a strong believer that everything happens for a reason. I am still intending to achieve as much as I can and will hopefully still be able to study medicine at university. If not, I'm sure I'll find another occupation that will be even more suitable for me."

That last paragraph demonstrates such a terrific attitude and I love it. A positive attitude is so important. Despite getting knocked down by COVID-19, Annalise is not going to let it define her future. Annalise is not staying down and giving up. She is coming out fighting! This will not dictate her future. She will not let society judge her for something that was out of her control. There is a place in the world for everyone and Annalise is going to make sure she achieves the best she can. I believe she will do it too.

CHAPTER 14 – PASSION

Steve Jobs once said:

"The only way to do great work is to love what you do."

Do something you are passionate about.

As our success in Dubai grew, management back in London could see what we had built and decided they would give us more countries to run. Our business that spanned the Middle East and Africa now had the jewel in the continent of Africa added to it! South Africa! This was great! Our business was expanding, and our success was growing. I had many a happy trip to Johannesburg and Cape Town to visit our offices and what a wonderful country South Africa is. My trips to South Africa for the bank inspired me to take my wife and kids there on holiday in 2016. I had to share this remarkable country with them. We all agreed that of all the countries we had visited, South Africa was on the verge of knocking Thailand from our number one holiday ever list!

However, around the same time we were given South Africa, we also got Pakistan. Pakistan had always been run by the Asian side of the bank, but one day they decided that Pakistan was not in Asia, it was in the Middle East!

Culturally, politically and geographically Pakistan is part of Asia. I scratched my head on this one and could not work out why Pakistan had been given to us.

Everything became apparent over the next few weeks when we were able to look through the books and take a closer look at our operation in Pakistan. It was not making any money but worse than that, it was actually costing money! What better way to get rid of the cost than by redrawing the map of the world and dumping it on me, I thought! However, the choice had been made from further up the chain and we had to get on with it.

Whichever way I looked at that business I just could not see how we were going to make a go of it. That was, until I met the two traders from our Karachi office. I wasn't keen to go to Pakistan as it wasn't the safest place in the world for British citizens at that time. Richard would go anywhere in the world if I asked him, but even he said: "Piss off" when I asked: "Fancy a trip to Pakistan?"

I decided there was no way I was putting my safety at risk for a business I could not see an upside in, and so we did the next best thing. We invited our traders to visit us in Dubai. Naturally they jumped at the chance and this is when I first had the pleasure of meeting Shoaib Shaikh.

Shoaib was a young guy who hadn't been in the bank for long but was passionate about Pakistan and the business. He was the junior on the desk, but he may as well have been running the show. He was very knowledgeable about the Pakistan market and assured me we could make a lot of money. I really wasn't seeing it, but he was adamant.

Back in London there had been talk from management about cutting our losses and shutting the Pakistan operation down but here was this kid telling me we could make a lot of money from Pakistan. His passion convinced me and in turn I convinced London to give it some time and see how it goes.

In our first year, we made a small profit. Nothing to shout from the rooftops but it was a start. Doubts about the business were still on the table in London but in Karachi the boys were all fired up and eager to get the next year underway.

Shoaib's passion never wavered. He would call me every day, even if there was nothing to talk about, just to keep my attention and tell me to have faith in the business and that better things would come. Sure enough, in the second year they bagged a huge deal that increased our profits by 500% - now that was something to shout about!

The Pakistan business still continues to this day and Shoaib is still there, making money! When we were on the verge of throwing the towel in and shutting it down, Shoaib's passion shone through and triumphed!

If you truly believe in something, champion it with passion. People notice passion. It makes others sit up and listen. They naturally want to know what you are so passionate about and why, and that secures their attention. If you are ambitious and passionate about something you will do it to the best of your ability.

Do something you are passionate about!

I did eventually go to Pakistan for a visit and I will tell you about that adventure a little later. It really does highlight the 'Doing Extra' category!

IMPACT STATEMENT: CORMAC

Cormac was due to sit his final A Level exams in English, Religious Studies and Sociology

"In all honesty Simon, I'm over the fricking moon about this. When I first heard about it I didn't believe it and had many struggles actually knowing what was going on as for a week there was complete uncertainty.

I think the best way to see how it affected our year group was through what happened on those last two days. As we all went home on the Friday the decision was to be made at 5pm so we had to find out after school. On the Friday, it had been a normal day no different to any other, all working towards getting results. The pressure of exams was still there as there had been talk of bringing the exams forward. So then, for that evening to be told all that was gone was a strange feeling.

I'd genuinely say it's the only time I've been unable to describe or show how I felt as I didn't really know what to feel or think. At first, I can remember my inherent laziness and lack of motivation to do anything revolving around school meant I felt great about this as it meant I could be lazy and do nothing, as I like to do. But it was only after thinking beyond this I started to see the negatives.

For me the fact my exams will be judged off my previous assessments and all is fine. I think they were genuine proof of how I would do in the exam or how I would have done similar to the exams. I can't fully comment yet as obviously, we haven't had our results back. But I think the issue many found was the fact they wouldn't be able to prove this and because we wouldn't sit the exams that our A-Levels would be considered less legitimate.

These concerns were clearly affecting peoples mental state on those two days. We had gone from being hard at work to suddenly having nothing to do. I think for me the worst part was knowing that suddenly I'd have two days left with people who had played a big part in my life.

I had known that day would come when the course finished. We'd all say bye and go our ways, but it was the abruptness of this that really hadn't settled in.

Those last two days had to be the quietest I had seen our whole year group through-out our time at school. I can re-call being in the study room with my mate Luke and we all just sort of sat there and didn't really say anything until he asked "Why the hell aren't we happy?" which seemed fair as again no one knew what to do or say.

I think because of this I am generally unhappy about the decision to not go ahead. Not for the academic reasons but for social reasons as there are many people I know I was only friends with because we went to the same school which I doubt will last outside. I feel we have lost the social aspect everyone talks of when finishing exams.

Regarding the question about how I feel the future may be affected, I don't feel any difference will be made in terms of our appearance to future employers. As far as it goes for the future I'm certain in what I want to do and I don't feel this will affect it, if anything it's helped me prepare. I aspire to be a Pilot and plan on joining the RAF after a year out, in which I plan on working on cars.

This extra time has helped me if anything. It has offered me many more opportunities in other areas. For example, I'm now taking a course in Aerospace Structure and Materials, which is something I actually want to pursue. I have also volunteered as a first responder for the NHS with the current epidemic as this gives purpose to my days I now have that are free. Without something to do I think I would struggle with keeping well mentally and physically.

So overall I feel the cancellation of the exams has really helped me, although the reasoning is tragic. I feel this cancellation of exams has ultimately helped me greatly as I can now do something which actually matters to me. I find school has never really suited me as this way of learning isn't helping me and has never really made me interested. Now I'm actively helping out and taking courses I'm interested in. I'm much happier and find greater meaning to daily activities. I have motivation to carry them out."

Clearly Cormac's main passion was not school. That is not to say he did not apply himself to the task. His education was a vessel to get him to where he wants to be, to get him to where his passion lies.

COVID-19 is not going to stand in his way. His passion lies in flying and joining the RAF. He has not sat back and wallowed in his "inherent laziness and lack of motivation to do anything revolving around school". Cormac has reflected on the situation and then asked himself a question:

"What is the next step that gets me to my passion?"

And he has answered his own question by starting a course in Aerospace Structure and Materials. He is not wasting his time, waiting for COVID-19 to deal him out his A Level grades and dictate which path he takes next. His passion is steering him to his next goal and I wish him well.

CHAPTER 15 – LISTENING

How many times have you heard your teachers say:

"God gave you two ears and only one mouth, so let's have more listening and less talking."

To be fair to my teachers they were justified. Every school report my parents received would have glowing comments in every subject. Describing my effort as first class. Stating my attitude in class was great and what a pleasure it was to teach me. However, every subject would conclude with: "Simon does tend to talk too much." I am still guilty of that to this day if the truth be known. I make good conversation. I contribute valuable and reasoned points when discussing a topic, but my wife does tend to switch off after I have hammered home the same point for the fifth time! But, one thing I discovered very early on in the working world was that listening was a lot more valuable to me.

When I first showed up in the world of finance, I did not have all the skills necessary to get me to where I ended up 25 years later. I had to learn those skills and the way to do that was by listening to people I could learn from.

Your life is not long enough to learn everything you need to know from scratch without help and that is why it pays to listen. Other people have skills and knowledge that can be very helpful to you if you take the time to listen.

It can be frustrating as a young person having to listen to old farts telling you what to do. When I was younger, if I had a problem I would go to my dad and ask for his opinion. Often what he had to say wasn't what I wanted to hear. I thought I knew best and he was out of touch. My dad would tell me how to fix the problem but I would brush that off and go out and tackle the problem my way. Eventually my way would not work and I would go back and do it the way my dad had told me to do it. To his credit he never said "told you so," he was just pleased to see I had solved my problem. I later realized he wasn't advising me in an effort to control me or to prove a point, he was trying to help me with the benefit of his years of experience.

We are all learning every day of our lives.

As the saying goes:

"The wise man knows he knows nothing, the fool thinks he knows all."

It is very easy to get caught up in yourself, in your own success or problems and not hear what is going on around you.

Earlier, I mentioned we had built the number one franchise in the Nigerian Foreign Exchange and Bond market globally. In 2010, and for the next few years, Nigeria was a magnet for investors. The country was sitting on huge amounts of oil at a time when the price of oil was soaring. Returns in Nigeria were fantastic and we made a lot of money for our clients and for the bank. What could go wrong?

We were sitting right in the middle of a massive bull market. A bull market is one where prices are rising which encourages investment and makes prices rise even more. Bull markets are the easiest markets to make money in if you know what you're doing!

But then, around 2014 the price of oil started to drop and the political arena in Nigeria turned negative. To start with, we did nothing. The returns in Nigeria still outweighed the risks of oil prices coming down. The oil slump could have just been a market 'correction' before taking off again and hitting new highs. Our colleagues in Russia thought we were getting nervous. Russia again was a big oil producer and a fall in the price of oil would have an impact on their market too.

We had a lot invested in Nigeria at the time and if the markets suddenly took a massive hit it would wipe us out completely. It was time to cut our investments and walk away. Richard wasn't so keen to do this. He was still adamant that Nigeria was the second largest economy on the continent of Africa, and he believed they could weather the storm. I wasn't so sure. Financial markets, especially in the emerging world - as was the case for Nigeria - are always looking for the next indicator to move and sometimes they react on things that really don't make sense, but when one goes, they all go!

A bear market is one where prices are falling which discourages investment and instead encourages more selling. The one thing every trader dreads is a bear market when things crash. Trading a bear market is an art. The secret is not to try and make money. The secret is not to lose money. If you can come out of a bear market with your bank balance intact, you have done a good job.

I had traded bear markets before and so I understood this, but Richard hadn't. Up until that point in his career, he had only traded on rallying bull markets where everybody makes money. If you're losing money in a bull market it's time to think about switching jobs!

Richard and I had many discussions on this regarding our Nigerian investments and being the boss, my decision was final. It was time to sell up and move on. The risk was too great. Richard didn't agree but the choice had been made and he started to reduce our investments slowly. Slowly, because he did not believe in selling up. He was waiting for the market to turn and prove his point.

In the summer of 2014 Richard and Nadine both went on their annual summer holiday and it was left to Ali, our other junior trader and me to hold the fort. The price of oil started to take a dive and the political situation in Nigeria was heating up. We made a snap decision. Get out now!

In two days Ali and I cut the position all the way to zero, which was a remarkable achievement given what was happening in the oil market. We had lost some money in cutting the position, but this was nothing compared to what we could have lost when the Nigerian market crashed a week later. We got out by the skin of our teeth.

When Richard came back he breathed a sigh of relief and told me he had not listened properly when we were talking about bear markets and how they could destroy you. I did not blame Richard; we all make mistakes and he was the first one to admit he had not seen it coming. Richard had been so caught up in the bull market of Nigeria he forgot to listen when the warnings were coming our way from other markets.

After that, Richard would joke that the best thing he had done in Nigeria was go on holiday! Ali laughed and told us all that he would never go on holiday again because we couldn't be trusted! I sat back and reflected on a lesson learned by everybody. The clues and market indicators were there. The markets were telling us to get out of our investments. All we had to do was listen. Always listen.

In the years before I went to work in Dubai, another incident highlighted the importance of listening. This one was a big benefit to me, but a friend of mine did not do so well.

I married Alison in 2000. Not long after, some friends of ours came over for lunch one Sunday on their way to catch a flight to Dubai from Heathrow airport.

Lisa is one of Alison's best friends and her husband is Bud. His real name is Chris but everybody calls him Bud. Bud had also worked in the financial markets for a broking house.

Remember, broking houses sat between the banks bringing them all the best prices for their deals. It's a little bit like a car insurance company. They don't insure your car directly but they get the best deals from the insurers and bring them to you so you don't have to contact the insurers direct and you get the best deal to insure your car.

Bud had been a broker for a few years but then the markets changed. A lot of the pricing went on to electronic platforms so there wasn't as much need for human intervention. Bud left the broker house and with his wife Lisa went on to set up their own Foreign Exchange company, utilising all the contacts and relationships they had made in their time in the city.

Bud was and still is a very upbeat guy. Nothing ever gets him down and he always has a positive outlook on life. The reason Bud was on his way to catch a flight to Dubai was because he was off to invest his money out there.

The Rulers of Dubai had decided they would build The Palm. This was an ambitious project which would take many years to complete, if they could complete it at all! The Palm was going to be a man-made island reclaimed from the sea with 5-star hotels and residential villas and apartments. It was the first phase in transforming Dubai into the huge metropolis that it is today.

The way Bud talked about Dubai was infectious. He was convinced that Dubai would become a mega city attracting business and tourism alike. An early investment would return huge amounts of money in the future. I hadn't even heard about Dubai at the time, let alone been there, but in a few short hours over a wonderful Sunday roast, Bud convinced Alison and I to invest in some property there as well. Bud went off to Dubai and put down the deposit on a couple of apartments for us on the not-yet-built The Palm Jumeirah! I was worried I would never see the money again and immediately booked a holiday to Dubai to go and see for myself what we had invested in.

The building of The Palm started in 2001 and we took delivery of our apartments in late 2006. By the time we got our hands on the keys the value of these apartments had tripled. It had been a long wait, but the return was worth it. Dubai had been on a six-year property boom. House prices went through the roof as more and more businesses set up there and tourism took off. Bud had seen this boom coming and thankfully I listened to him.

There was just one problem. I was watching the financial markets of Dubai and things were not looking so great. The markets were telling me that a shock was on the way. The financial markets tend to be ahead of the man on the street by some months. When the country is looking great the financial markets are more likely to see any downturn coming, first. Dubai had boomed too quickly and the markets were telling me this. I felt a crash was coming. I put my apartments up for sale and within a week I had people wanting to buy them. I told Bud it was time to get out and a crash was coming, but he was in love with the place.

He told me on several occasions:

"Dubai is the land of milk and honey. You're making a big mistake selling up and getting out."

I listened to the markets and sold my apartments and was very satisfied with my trebled profits. That was more than good enough for me. Bud stayed invested and sure enough the market crashed. From 2007 until 2010, Dubai's economy went badly wrong. It was a classic economic boom and bust cycle. The markets had rallied too fast and the economy could not sustain it.

Unfortunately, Bud lost a lot of money and regretted not listening to the warning signs I was telling him I could see.

Don't worry about Bud though! Bud being Bud, he bounced right back and went on to bigger and better things. You can't fault his attitude. Knock him down and he will get right back up again. If you ever want to chat to a pair of serial entrepreneurs who can turn water in to wine, go find Bud and Lisa.

To this day, whenever I am with Bud and he introduces me to somebody, the first thing he tells them is:

"This fella could have saved me a lot of money, but I didn't listen."

Never underestimate the value of listening. Other people have opinions and knowledge that might benefit you. That is not to say that everybody's opinions and knowledge will be best for you. Generally I discount 50% of everything I hear until I have had the time to do my own research and collate my own thoughts on the topic. People sometimes have hidden agendas or an unintentional bias when they talk. That could mean that what they're telling me might not be right for my specific circumstances, so I reserve the right to make up my own mind.

Take what you hear and do your own research so that you can make an informed decision. If you ask two different traders the best way to trade they may have differing methods to recommend. One of those methods might be right for you, and both – or neither - may work for you. You might find that a combination of the two may be the best approach for you. No matter the topic, take what you hear and do your own research to come to an informed conclusion.

Listening is a great skill. It's free and you have it.

IMPACT STATEMENT: ALICE

Alice was due to sit her final A Level exams in Chemistry, Biology and Math's.

"When the coronavirus first came about, I had a gut feeling that I wouldn't have to sit my exams which was really weird but I never expected them to actually get cancelled.

On that Wednesday evening when Boris announced that there will be no summer exam series I initially was very relieved as I had become very stressed over the whole process of sitting the exams and worried that I would not achieve the grades I could, buckling under the immense pressure that I put myself under to succeed.

After thinking about it all, I was a bit skeptical as I didn't really know what was going to happen. I suddenly had 2 more days left at school which I emotionally hadn't prepared for. But now, I am happy that I do not have to sit any exams and that I now have no academic stresses for the next 6 months, but I am still unsure whether I could've achieved higher grades if I had sat the exams instead of my teachers awarding me a final grade which I think I could better.

I also thought about how in years to come, my qualifications will not be comparable to other people who actually sat the exam in previous years. Will it impact me in further study? Or will my grades be seen as a true reflection of my ability? The thing is, I have no idea. Nobody does at this moment in time. It worries me as I have no say in the matter, but hopefully my teachers know me well enough as an individual to give me the appropriate grade that I theoretically should've gone on to achieve had I sat the summer exams.

The end of my A levels would've not only marked my time at the end of education but also my time at my high school. I loved everything about my school and I don't think that the abrupt ending was what we all were prepared for. Usually there is a Leaver's Ball, Leaver's Day and a special lunch with all teaching staff and upper sixth, but we didn't get any of that. There was no celebration of our time together which seems very unfair but I know that we will have some sort of Ball at the end of the whole pandemic but we do not know when that will be.

Overall, I am relieved that I do not have to study for my A levels anymore but being stuck inside all day kind of makes me wish I was still studying for the exams. I am very bored but that soon goes when I find something good to watch on Netflix "

Alice's concern about how her qualifications will be viewed in the future has been a common theme I have been hearing from most young people. As Alice states, at this point nobody knows, but this is why we must not dwell on it. Who knows if future employers will regard you differently because you were "given" your grades as many people like to point out.

I've had plenty of experience hiring young people in the finance industry over the last 25 years, and I've never focused on grade results or the associated subjects taken. I was always far more interested in the person. I wanted to identify candidates I could mold in to a great trader. I wanted to find hungry, energetic and passionate people.

School and university do not actively equip young people with the traits and attributes I look for in a candidate. They don't teach potential traders how to trade foreign exchange, equities, bonds etc. They don't teach them how the financial systems work on a day-to-day basis or about risk management or value at risk or leverage. It would save a hell of a lot of time in the world of trading if they did and I am sure there are many, varied business owners out there echoing my thoughts.

Some careers require a specialist learning path: doctors for instance. Personally, I wouldn't be too happy if I was laying on the operating table only for my "surgeon" to tell me I was their first ever operation and they had just graduated from the university of nowhere with a degree in film studies. But there are many industries out there who need a skill set which is just not being taught. How about we introduce a course in Financial Trading?

The point I am trying to make is, when will the education system cooperate and consult with corporate industry leaders to determine the skills they need from school leavers and university graduates? What do employers require of young people to add value? How can the education system equip them with all of the relevant skills to enter the work place of their choice and make a valuable contribution?

However, let's not put all the blame at the feet of the education system. The corporate world needs to be knocking on doors of institutions and learning centres and saying: "This is what we need! This is the skill set we need you to provide our future employees with!"

CHAPTER 16 - DOING EXTRA

Back when we were talking about passion, I mentioned that I eventually did make a trip to Pakistan. The next topic is 'Doing Extra' so now is an ideal time to tell you about it.

Like I said, when we 'inherited' the Pakistan business I was not too keen to make a trip down to Karachi as it was an unsafe place to visit at the time. I did read a short while ago that things have improved now which is great. Karachi has dropped from the 6th most dangerous place to visit in the world to 70th according to the World Crime Index published in 2019.

Richard, in his Army days had been to some of the most dangerous places in the world so when he said "No" to Karachi, it didn't exactly fill me with confidence to get on a plane. Shoaib had told me about the time he and his wife had been held up at gunpoint sitting at a set of traffic lights in Karachi, robbed of their money and possessions. This was a regular occurrence for the population of Karachi! What was not a regular occurrence in Karachi was what happened next in Shoaib's robbery. Shoaib's wife asked the gunman if he would give them back their identification cards. She reasoned with him that they were no good to him and getting replacements was a real pain in the arse. The gunman looked at them both and paused for a few moments. He then gave Shoaib and his wife ALL of their money and possessions back, went to the car directly behind Shoaib's and proceeded to rob them instead! A gunman with a heart? You be the judge.

Another favourite pastime of the well-respected Karachi criminal at the time was kidnap. Kidnapping visitors from the West for ransom was a popular earner back then! However, Shoaib bugged me to visit and eventually I reluctantly agreed.

It was only a short plane ride from Dubai to Karachi so I decided I could manage a day trip. Safety in numbers sprang to mind and I told Ali, our junior trader he was coming with me as it would, "broaden his horizons!" (Yeah, right!) We then went on to invite our business manager Jamie on our little adventure.

Flights were booked and the internal security of the bank sent us a lovely email about how we were going to a "very dangerous" place and we should be on our guard and vigilant at all times! They went on to say that casual clothing rather than the standard banking uniform of a suit and tie would be more appropriate. If we rocked up in a suit, we could be seen as lucrative targets for kidnap and ransom! Oh, I was so looking forward to this trip! I did find myself wondering at the time that if I was kidnapped, how much the bank might be prepared to pay for my safe return. What was I worth?

We were also told we would be met by an armed security team at the airport who would transport us in a bulletproof vehicle to the bank. What on earth were we doing?

When we landed in Karachi we were met by the security boys and escorted to our 4x4 for the long ride into the heart of Karachi. When we got to the car, the security guy opened the back door for Ali to get in. I walked around the car to the other side and started to open the heavy bulletproof door. The security guy came flying around the car and went nuts! He was shouting at me whilst escorting me back to the other side of the car. What did I do so wrong that prompted him to go mental at me? Turns out that he was worried somebody might shoot me if he was not shielding me! Personally, I thought this was a bit over the top and he was making a right song and dance about nothing. Turns out, he wasn't.

We all piled into the back seat. Ali sat on the left, Jamie on the right and I sat in the middle. The middle was the most uncomfortable seat and Jamie said as I was the boss, he should take the middle seat and I should take his window seat. I insisted that I was fine in the middle and off we went.

About halfway into the journey Jamie brought up our seating arrangements again and then worked out why I had insisted on remaining in the middle. Jamie was a large chap at the time and was always telling me he really needed to go on a diet and lose some weight.

Jamie turned to me and said:

"You sat in the middle because you know that if a bullet manages to penetrate this armored car it would have to go through me before it got to you?"

I looked at Jamie and let's just say my body language didn't contradict his statement! That is exactly why I had chosen to sit in the middle. Jamie was fine with it. He was convinced that any bullet would come through Ali's side first. These terrorists had learnt their Green Cross Code and would hardly be standing in the middle of the road when we passed by. They would make sure they were safe from cars by standing on the pavement! If you say so Jamie! Ali pointed out that him sitting on the left would do me no favours if we were shot at. Ali was so skinny that if he turned sideways you wouldn't see him!

As the day went on, I realized why the security guy had got so steamed up about me diverting away from his security plan. We had not been in the office that long when a 'small' bomb blew up outside the mosque next door to the bank. Nobody in the office even raised an eyebrow while Ali, Jamie and I ducked under a desk! In the evening, just after our plane had taken off from Karachi for the short flight back to Dubai, terrorists stormed the cargo area of the airport terminal and shot at the planes behind us! Hence why I think this story sits quite well in the 'Doing Extra' chapter.

Our visit to the office in Karachi showed the people who worked there that we were serious about their business and keeping them open. They went on to bag that big deal I talked about and the rest is history. Sometimes in life you have to do things you don't want to do. There are times when you really don't want to risk it and go that extra mile. But putting that little bit extra into everything you do can result in bigger returns and greater success, not only for you but for others too.

Obviously that example of doing extra is not an everyday occurrence.

Back in Chapter 11 I shared my experience of applying for the role of junior trader and my promotion from back office boy just 3 months after joining the financial trading world. At the time I felt as if I had truly made it! I was ready to trade and prove to everybody that I was the next big shot in the city! I was pumped but the reality was far from glamorous!

For the first year I was the lowest of the low on the trading floor. I was responsible for getting breakfast and lunch for the traders every day. I had to get the teas and coffees, and drop suits off at the dry cleaners while I was getting everybody's lunch. Every mundane task and errand that needed doing was given to me so that the traders could focus on their job.

On one occasion I actually spent the majority of the day standing on the pavement outside the bank. My boss at the time had just taken delivery of a brand new Aston Martin and he decided he would park it in a space right outside the bank so that everybody could see it. My job that day was to make sure the parking meter was constantly filled with pound coins so he did not get a ticket and also to watch over his car and gauge reactions of people. By the middle of the afternoon the boss decided he had done enough showing off and I could return to the backlog of mundane tasks that were waiting for me. I was told to take the car around to the car park at the back of the bank and come in. As I went back outside to move the car a rather smartly dressed city chap in a pin striped suit and a bowler hat came down the road. I would have put him around 50 to 60 years old and quite clearly somebody who had spent a long time in the city. As he got to the Aston Martin he stopped to admire this beautiful machine. I walked forward and stood next to him looking at the car.

"What a magnificent car that is, I would love to be able to afford one of those," the bowler hatted chap said to me.

I turned to him and replied "It is rather nice isn't it?"

I then took the car key out of my pocket and pressed the unlock button. The Aston beeped and the indicator lights flashed. I walked around to the driver's side, opened the door and as I got in to the car I looked at him and said:

"Work hard and play hard son, that's my motto!"

As I started up the car and drove off the look on his face was priceless. I could see him trying to figure out how this young lad could afford a brand new Aston Martin. What did he do? What was the bank paying him? His face said it all!

After hours of boredom, I decided to make the most of the situation and have a little fun, and thinking about it now still brings a smile to my face. I knew I wasn't going to be on the bottom rung of the ladder forever. If I worked hard and put in the extra mile, I would soon move up on the trading floor.

In those early years I did all of the boring and mundane jobs and often before anybody asked. I could have complained and I'm sure others in my place would have. I was employed as a junior trader for the bank not some errand boy! It wasn't in my contract to get Dave a sausage sandwich (brown sauce on white bread) every morning and it certainly wasn't in my contract to get that curry stain off Gav's suit jacket! But I did it.

And I did it to the best of my ability.

I made sure I was the first one in the office every morning, to see that everything was in place for the traders to come in and get trading. Were the computers all turned on and working? Were all the phone lines to the brokers working?

I also made sure I was the last one to leave the office in the evening just in case anybody needed something. I wanted to prove myself and my way of doing that was to make sure I went that extra mile to make the office function effectively and efficiently. Over time, my hard work and extra effort paid off. My boss was impressed, as were his traders and eventually I earned my own seat at the trading desk. I had proven to everybody that I had what they wanted. They all saw in me the value I could bring to them by doing extra!

CHAPTER 17 – PREPARATION

"By failing to prepare, you are preparing to fail."

That's a saying from Benjamin Franklin that I heard from my teacher's countless times growing up. I didn't take much notice of it at the time. It was just another soundbite teachers came out with in order to make you do something.

I did not fail my GCSE's or A Levels, in fact I passed every exam I sat. But with just a little more preparation, I know I could have scored higher grades. My method of revising was to sit in my parent's dining room with all my books open, listening to the radio. I looked very busy to my mum and dad when they walked past the room and once I explained to them that the songs of Queen were beneficial to my learning because my revision then got a rhythm to it. Well it was Bohemian Rhapsody and We Are the Champions all day long from then on in!

In reality, I could have done better with some prepared revision strategies rather than open the books and crank up the volume. I passed my exams but as Charlie will happily tell you, his GCSE results were better than mine and therefore he is smarter than me. I can also now confirm that his A Level results are better than mine. He has just received his grades. Charlie got A, B, B in his A Levels. I am feeling VERY proud of my boy!

To be fair, he is smarter than me because he prepared for his GCSE's and A Levels. He did not prepare for COVID-19 though, how could he? How could anybody have prepared for COVID-19? But he was prepared for the A Level course and what it entailed. Prepared to work hard, to learn and to put the effort in. So, when COVID-19 cancelled the exams, Charlie was in a good position as a direct result of that preparation.

Back in Dubai, I was once asked to attend a meeting that had absolutely nothing to do with my business. A different department in the bank had a client coming in for a meeting and they wanted to develop a relationship with them for future business opportunities. They asked me to pop in halfway through the meeting as the boss of their department was away on vacation at the time and I was the only Senior Executive present in the bank on that day. The idea being that a Senior Executive wanting to pop in and shake hands with the client halfway through would be a big boost to the client's ego! Yeah sure, whatever.

Half an hour into the meeting I got a telephone call letting me know it was time to pop along to the meeting room so off I trotted. When I opened the door, I could tell instantly that the meeting wasn't going well. The meeting room had a long table in the centre, which could sit 10 people either side of it. Down one side of the table were nine of our finest brains from Structuring, Sales and Research. On the opposite side was one very uncomfortable looking client! Yes, just one person from the client side! It looked like I had walked into an episode of 'Strictly come banking!' In the middle of 'the judges' was an empty chair, which had been designated for me, as the Senior Executive of the bank, to take and my colleagues did not hesitate inviting me to sit in it!.

Very calmly, I walked around to the other side of the table and sat next to the client ignoring my nine finest colleagues. I then proceeded to introduce myself and ask the client how he was and how long he was in Dubai for. Five minutes later, after we had enjoyed our introduction and discovered a bit about each other I acknowledged my colleagues and let them continue. Every one of them was keen to tell this client exactly what they could do for him and put their pitch forward admirably.

The client sat there, quietly taking all this information in, but I could tell something was wrong. Eventually I interrupted the information onslaught coming from the other side of the table and asked the client a very simple question:

"What can we do for you?"

If we'd known this up front, the meeting could have been tailored with the relevant people in the room to answer the client's questions. This would have saved him – and us – precious time but unfortunately nobody had bothered to prepare for this client or the meeting.

I have attended countless meetings like the above in my career. Meetings just like this one where a little preparation could have avoided a wasted journey and saved precious time and resources.

The lesson here is, a little preparation can go a long way to making a client feel as though their needs are being adequately met and valuable time is saved on both sides.

IMPACT STATEMENT: KATIA

Katia was due to sit her IB exams studying English Literature, Psychology, Business Studies, Maths, Biology and Spanish.

"Initially, when I heard the exams that were due to take place in May would be cancelled, I was extremely disappointed. I had worked so hard for the past two years and had consolidated all of my notes for nothing. Exams were really important to me as it determined my choice of university as all my offers were conditional to specific grade requirements. However, I have since realised that there are bigger issues going on around the world and exams having gone forward would have not only have been insensitive to those struggling but also so utterly pointless. Everyone in some way shape or form has been affected by this, whether it be personally infected or abiding by the laws under self-isolation.

I am not too worried about how my grades will be determined as I know I have worked really hard throughout the whole year and I know that my school would not permit me to be awarded grades that did not meet my ability. If anything, I find it even more frustrating as it makes university acceptance more competitive with the increased likelihood of everyone meeting their requirements/predictions and risk their course being oversubscribed.

A lot of people in the years above me have had no sympathy for my year group at all. They complained that it was unfair that we did not have to take exams like they had to, but had they been in our situation they would be thinking very differently.

If exams were to go ahead, I would be struggling. From attending online lessons, the quality is not of the same standard as lessons being taught in the classrooms. Alongside poor internet connection and technological issues, the communication between myself and my teacher has proved to be difficult. In this aspect, I am extremely happy that I don't have exams to prepare for as I know it would make me even more stressed.

Although many people complain that we are the 'lucky' year group, there are many things my year will miss out on. From graduation, to prom, to grad trip and muck-up day, we won't get to experience some iconic events which we have always dreamed of attending. It's upsetting when I think of my last day of school, as I did not treat it as such. My last day of school was advertised as our last day of term two and the start of the Easter holidays, not my last day of school ever.

I know that when this is all over my friends and I will celebrate together, however it may not be on a beach in Bali, but instead on a House Party or Zoom call. It's really an unfortunate situation, but in the grand scheme of things I just hope this pandemic is resolved soon and our lives can try and go back to the way they once were."

———————————————

I really understand Katia's frustration about not getting to sit the exams, having worked so hard for two years. You feel like you have been cheated. You have dedicated your time and effort to these exams and made sacrifices to get the work done, but there is no closure. To top it all off everybody around you who isn't in your situation is moaning because they had to sit exams and weren't "given" their qualifications. Let's make one thing clear. Nobody is being given their qualifications. The effort, attitude, work ethic, passion and sacrifice you have put in to your studies over the years is being graded. Just because you did not get to condense those years of work in to a 2 hour exam does not disqualify you. COVID-19 wasn't your fault. It has happened and WE ALL have to deal with it.

COVID-19 for me has highlighted the need for change in the education system. Why are we judging our young people on a handful of exams at the end of a lengthy course? Some people breeze through exams, while other students can't handle them at all. It does not make them any different in their ability to learn and be an integral member of society. Let's change the way we assess and "judge" our young people. In fact let's ask the question: "What exactly are we judging in the current education format?" Is it fair to determine the path of our young people based on a 2-hour exam that was sat in a stuffy, hot hall or gymnasium?

And then we wonder why there is a rising mental health issue in our young people? Pressure, pressure, pressure and most of it completely pointless!

CHAPTER 18 - THE WORLD NEEDS YOU

So we have covered our "10 things that require zero talent or money"

1. Being on time – don't be late and use your time wisely, you don't know how much of it you have left.

2. Work ethic – are you professional in what you do? Are you reliable? Do you get the job done? Adopt a work ethic that befits your product. Somebody is always watching.

3. Effort – People notice effort. Effort is like a price tag; it demonstrates the added value you can bring to your clients.

4. Body language – how you 'hold' yourself makes a statement without you even speaking. Your facial expressions can tell a story without you even opening your mouth.

5. Energy – Max nailed it.
"Everyone has a choice in this situation, to be sluggish and demotivated, or to get up off your arse and do something productive and grow as a human…….."
Enough said!

6. Attitude - "Do not judge me by my successes, judge me by how many times I fell down and got back up again."
Your attitude speaks volumes. A positive attitude will get results.

7. Passion – Do the things you are passionate about. If you are ambitious and passionate about something you will do it to the very best of your ability.

8. Listening - "The wise man knows he knows nothing, the fool thinks he knows all."

Your life is not long enough to learn everything you need to know from scratch without help and that is why it pays to listen. Take the things you hear, investigate, research and reach your own conclusion.

9. Doing extra - putting that little bit extra into everything you do can result in bigger returns and greater success, not only for you but for others too.

10. Preparation – a little preparation can go a long way and save you a lot of time. By failing to prepare, you are preparing to fail.

COVID-19 has sent shock waves throughout the world. Many economies are struggling. Some industries and businesses are on the verge of ruin. Never have our younger generation been so important. The world needs you and future generations to sort this mess out. The world needs YOU! We need you to shape the future, to rebuild our world and drag us out the other side of COVID-19.

I have a few more life hacks and tips that I am going to share with you in addition to our "ten things that require zero talent or money".

I have no doubt that if you employ these hacks and tips in your everyday life, you will be well on your way to a promising career in your chosen field. Not only that, it'll also set you up for life, and help those around you to succeed and flourish.

CHAPTER 19 - STOP DOING POINTLESS CRAP!

So, you have evaluated why you want to start a business, created a mission statement and worked out what a start-up needs. As a start-up we have covered ten things that require zero talent or money to employ in the YOU company. YOU have all of those things and need to put them into practice in order to deliver maximum value to your clients. Your clients are not employing you to add little to no value, so start by cutting out anything that has no value.

Have you heard of Candy Crush? Candy Crush was born in 2012 and it even has a Wikipedia entry:

"In the game, players complete levels by swapping coloured pieces of candy on a game board to make a match of three or more of the same colour, eliminating those candies from the board and replacing them with new ones, which could potentially create further matches. Matches of four or more candies create unique candies that act as power-ups with larger board-clearing abilities. Boards have various goals that must be completed within a fixed number of moves or limited amount of time, such as a certain score or collecting a specific number of a type of candy."[1]

I played Candy Crush religiously for seven years. Five lives a day minimum play time! Five free lives when I woke up, five free lives before I went to sleep. I reached level 2046. Impressed? I was, until one day in December 2019. On that day I deleted

---

[1] "Candy Crush Saga"
Wikipedia, Wikimedia Foundation, 6 September 2020
https://en.wikipedia.org/wiki/Candy_Crush_Saga.

Candy Crush from my iPad. In fact, I deleted every game on my phone and iPad. Why?

On that day in 2019 I had another revelation. I was driving Alex, my daughter to school. We were talking about her mock GCSE exams. Alex is not naturally gifted academically, just like I wasn't back in my school days. Alex has to work hard at her schoolwork and I am immensely proud of her for the effort she puts in, but like most teenagers she loves to have a moan about school:

"What's the point of GCSE's? What's the point of A Levels? We are taught stuff I will never use in my life. What's the point of learning it? There is just so much to learn, how do we fit it all in?"

I have to admit, I have some sympathy for the above statements to a degree. I do think that the education system could be updated to make it more relevant to the students of today and the need for a 21st Century workforce. The education system hasn't really changed since the introduction of free secondary education for all, around about the time of World War II. For me, schools are a little bit like a factory conveyor belt. You go in at one end when you're a toddler and are expected to come out the other end at 18, the finished product!

However, back to Alex and her moan on that morning. Your GCSE's are the keys that unlock A Levels, college or apprenticeships. A Levels are the keys that unlock University placements, etc. So, there is a reason why you do school exams. I'm not saying they are the be-all and end-all of life. Some very successful people have left school with very few - if any - qualifications, but they are the exception to the rule. Generally speaking, having some of these exams under your belt will make life easier in whatever you choose to do going forward. The key point being, there is a clear reason for doing exams and dedicating your time to studying for them.

Those who claim they don't have enough time, might not realise just how much time we spend on pointless crap. You can fit so much more into life if you stop doing stuff that is a waste of time and isn't relevant to furthering your business, YOU. Candy Crush never got me ahead in the bank. The act of playing Candy Crush never introduced me to a client that needed my expertise. Candy Crush was not relevant to me, but I was blind to that fact!

Instead of playing Candy Crush first thing every morning, I could have been looking at the financial markets, and working out what I was going to do that day. I could have used those 30 minutes playing Candy Crush to find out what had happened in Asia while I had been asleep, rather than wasting half an hour when I got to work to find out.

I am not dismissing Candy Crush, it's a bit of downtime for some people but all of these games and pointless apps on my phone and iPad were a distraction to ME. If I wanted some downtime, I could have meditated, written in a journal or done something physical that would have benefitted my overall health and wellbeing.

If I'm bored I could look at Google and educate myself about something I don't know. What's going to be more beneficial to me and potentially more interesting? Educating myself about something I know nothing about or reaching level 2047 on Candy Crush?

Picture this: I am at a social event. I have just been introduced to some people I have never met before. They seem quite interesting people. They have stuff to talk about. They have views on climate change, politics, sport, careers or any other topic you can imagine and might want to know more about. They turn to me and ask for my opinion on the subject they are discussing. I take a moment to consider my response. Shit, I don't know anything about the mating habits of the wild Alaskan mountain bear. What can I add without making myself look stupid?

"Well I can't speak for the wild Alaskan mountain bears and how frisky they get around this time of year, but I can tell you last night I hit 2047 on Candy Crush! Boom!"

At this point, there is an awkward silence. Time stands still. People slowly start talking amongst themselves and moving discreetly away from me. Conversation killer! It could even be a possible career killer for YOU! Why didn't I know about those fricking bears?

That's me making up an example. I am not saying you need to know about the mating habits of wild Alaskan mountain bears. I can't recall the mating habits of the wild Alaskan mountain bear ever coming up in conversation at a social gathering I have been at, but you get my point.[2]

You have at your fingertips the greatest source of research and education and it's called the internet! It's called Google!

When I was a kid we had to go to the library to research and find stuff and there was only a fraction of what you can find on the internet today. There is no excuse for you not to learn something new every day. Learn something that is going to help you develop and market YOUR product to the masses.

---

[2] Just for the record, in case it comes up in future gatherings you may find yourself at, bears normally mate in the spring to early summer time and give birth the following winter. You can have that one for nothing! Oh, and by the way, I Googled it!

When people say: "Oh there isn't enough time in the day," ask to see their mobile phones and check how many mind numbingly dumb games and apps they have on it!

As we discovered earlier, time is the most precious commodity you have. Why would you waste it on pointless pursuits which you gain nothing from?

In the case of Richard, he was told he was going to die from a brain tumour and the life expectancy of his condition was one year. He did not waste the precious time he had left on pointless things. He crammed in as many of the things he wanted to do before his time ran out.

Your time is also running out, but unlike Richard you don't know when it's coming to an end. If I told you, you had one year to live would you make sure you got that next level of Candy Crush beaten or would you go out and do the things you really wanted to do before your time came to an end? Just think about your time and what you really want to do with it, then cut out all the pointless exercises you do that wastes it.

I am not saying you shouldn't enjoy some downtime, some time to relax. I'm also not saying that Candy Crush and phone apps are the work of the devil. I've just come to realise they are no longer right for ME and I'm able to achieve so much more with that time than I did before. It's a personal choice. When I realised they were distracting me from all of the things I should be doing, and were just a complete time suck I stopped. And the best thing? I don't miss it!

That day, back in 2019, I sat in a hospital waiting room. I had to be there, no choice. I was on my phone playing Bricks n Balls. My weekly iPhone stats popped up on the screen and my screen time was massively up from the week before! This was all down to the new game, Bricks n Balls! I was using this game to 'kill time.' Killing time? Are you serious? Why would I want to kill time? I only have so much of it.

That was when the penny dropped! I put the phone away and picked up the local newspaper. I read all about the local candidates that were standing in the December 2019 General Election in my area. Time well spent seeing as I would have to vote for one of them in a few days' time. I found out what each of them would do if they were elected so I could make an informed choice when I went to vote. I can't moan about my local MP doing nothing for me if I have not bothered to find out what principles they are standing for and voted for them in the election based on zero knowledge.

Deleting all those games and apps that I did not need from my iPad and iPhone was a really liberating experience. The following day alone, I got so much more stuff done. I noticed a huge difference in my productivity. I wrote the outline for this chapter of the book for starters! I sorted out all the issues that were stacking up in my property company that I kept putting off. I had a conversation with my acting agent and got my headshots sent over to him for his new website. I went to the hospital to visit an old couple who have done so much for my family over the years and put a smile on their faces. Rather than cook fish fingers, chips and beans for dinner I put together a family favourite which I had not brought out the bag for ages: Herb crusted rack of lamb. I'm not the greatest cook in the world but I love doing it, and I found time to do it.

Since that day I have not played Candy Crush. I have not played Golf Challenge. And, I have not played Bricks n Balls. Do I feel better for it? Yes. Have I achieved so much more? Yes! Thanks for the conversation in the car Alex. I started telling you to cut out the rubbish in your day but in doing so, I realized how much pointless crap I was doing in my own day.

You have to remember that these games and activities are designed to keep your attention and get you addicted. I was able to identify that and admit they were the reason I wasn't getting stuff done. I hope you can learn from my example, and analyse your own time waster behaviours. Think about what you could be doing with the time you know you are wasting.

Put this book down for a minute. Pick your phone or tablet up and just go through all of your apps. Count up how many of them bring nothing meaningful to your life. How many of them are pointless and give you zero benefit? Make a change, delete the ones that you could very easily live without.

I dare you!

Don't waste your time. Stop doing meaningless, pointless crap that gets you nothing! Employ your time wisely.

Even when we are in the car Alex and I employ our time wisely. We have our best chats in the car about all kinds of topics. When it comes to my writing, Alex is kind of like my test ground for what I am working on. In addition to that, she's also a great example that what I am trying to do for young people also works for her.

It was the last week of school before the 2019 Christmas holidays and Alex had been taking some of her mock GCSE exams. Some had gone well, some could have gone better, but as we discussed mocks are very helpful in letting you know what you don't know, so not smashing them out of the park isn't the end of the world!

One subject where Alex struggles is math's. It is not her strongest subject and not one she enjoys. It's hard to get motivated for something you don't enjoy doing.

At the start of this final year we were looking at a grade 3 prediction for math's. Nothing wrong with grade 3. All the grades show achievement otherwise they would not be there. Look at it this way. If a grade 4 was a pass what would be the point of having 1, 2 or 3? You might as well not have them. 1, 2, 3, 4, 5, 6, 7, 8 and 9 all mean something. They all show achievement so don't think you have failed if you don't get a specific number (or above) in everything!

Back to Alex. So, she was predicted to get a grade 3 in math's, but to go on and do A Levels, which she wants to do, Alex needed a 5 in math's. Only one person could get that 5 and that is Alex.

The school put extra help in place for the pupils in all their subjects, including math's in the form of 'subject clinics.' These are sessions provided for pupils in various subjects that take place during the lunch break or after school.

Alex wasn't looking forward to the prospect of going to math's clinic and couldn't motivate herself for the challenge. How were we going to get from a 3 to a 5? Somehow, Alex needed to change her mindset towards the subject. I am not saying she needed to fall in love with math's, be its best friend 24/7 and send it flowers, but she needed to prepare herself for the challenge. Alex needed to realise that to go on to the next path in her dream journey (she wants to teach English to kids in Japan) grade 5 in math's is needed. We took a few of the '10 things that require zero talent or money' and talked about them. The point she responded to the most was cutting out useless crap. She used the extra time to focus on math's and attend the special clinics at school in the weeks leading up to Christmas. If you want something badly enough you have to work for it and Alex was putting in a consistent effort in order to achieve her desired result.

On the last day of term before the Christmas break Alex was surprised to receive the Sandra Fortune Cup for the most improved math's student. The Math's Department award this cup at the end of each term to recognise the student who has put the most effort in to turn their math's results around. Alex had no clue she was going to receive this award. The head of the Math's Department stood up and made his speech:

"This term the Sandra Fortune Cup is going to a student that has applied herself to math's and made a huge improvement. She has attended all the math's clinics and never once stopped asking questions. Her attitude, work ethic and doing the extra needed this term has been noticed by her teachers and she thoroughly deserves this award."

Alex nearly fell off her chair when her name was read out. She was genuinely shocked. Sometimes you put the effort in and think nobody is watching. Somebody is always watching!

When I picked her up from school, Alex was standing there proudly holding the cup for all to see.

At a parent's evening after Christmas, we learned her predicted grade for math's had risen from a 3 to a 5, with a good chance of getting a 6 if the hard work continued.

Alex had completely changed her mind set to math's. She realised she had to do that little bit extra. She had to apply herself with a positive attitude and a good work ethic if she wanted to embark on the next leg of her dream. Just making a few small changes has given her big results. I didn't change her. Her teachers did not change her. We offered advice and resources and she decided to make the change for herself. Making that change is a big ask because it takes you out of your comfort zone, but once you do it, you feel the benefit immediately. As the saying goes:

"You can take a horse to water, but you can't make it drink."

Making that change has really paid off for Alex and she has gained the recognition for this change.

As for me, well I have a smile on my face. The message I am trying to get across has worked and if it can work for Alex, it can work for anyone. Well done Alex. I am very proud of you!

CHAPTER 20 - TAKE OWNERSHIP

There exists a big problem in the corporate and political world. Many of the companies and political parties you know of have this problem. It's called the blame culture.

Do not let the blame culture infect YOU.

The morning after the General Election of 2019 we all woke up to find that it had resulted in a massive win for the conservative party. All the 'losing' politicians were on the TV blaming everybody else apart from themselves. Not one of them could take a long hard look in the mirror and acknowledge they had played some part in their loss. It was disappointing to see that these are the people who are supposed to lead the country and all they could do was pass the blame. What kind of message does that send to the public and your generation?

All through your education you learn it's ok to make mistakes as long as you acknowledge them and learn from them.

The message our politicians are sending out is:

"Make a mistake and then blame everybody else for it and you will go far."

NO, YOU WONT!

The blame culture in the corporate world is not new but I would say it has manifested itself a lot more strongly in the last 10 years or so. Certainly, in the banking world the blame culture really started to take off after the Global Financial Crisis (GFC) in 2008.

The GFC of 2008 took the banking world to the edge of collapse. In short, the world had been on a bull market run for almost a decade. Property prices kept going up and up and everybody wanted to cash in on this big rally in the markets. Everybody had a mortgage, and everybody kept borrowing more and more money to buy the property market which just kept climbing.

One of my personal assistants at one point owned three properties that she had no intention of keeping. She would buy a house and then immediately put it back on the market for say 10 or 20 thousand pounds more than she had paid for it. Over a period of about two years she must have bought and sold some 20 houses and all with money she did not have. The banks were letting her borrow amounts that she really could not afford to borrow on her salary and that was how the housing bubble became inflated.

The problem was that the increase in property prices and the huge amounts of debts people had built up to buy these properties with mortgages was not sustainable. As property prices went up so did the price of other commodities such as oil and gas. That made life more expensive for people as the inflation rates around the globe went up. As time went on, the gap between what people were earning and the debts they had to pay back got wider and wider until their income wasn't covering the mortgage repayments and meeting the cost of day to day living.

When that happened, people started trying to sell their properties and the prices began to drop.

As more and more people saw property prices coming down they all started trying to sell. Nobody wanted to be owning these properties when the housing market crashed.

The problem for the banks was that they had lent all the money to buy these houses. Now that the value of these houses was lower than the amounts the banks had loaned, the banks had a massive hole in their balance sheet.

It's a little more complicated than that, but that's the basics of what happened. Watch a film called The Big Short if you want to know more about the GFC. In short, the banking sector had to be bailed out by Governments printing money!

The housing crisis which started in the USA overflowed into Europe where they had a whole host of problems in the Eurozone. In this case countries were on the verge of going bankrupt!

Greece was in a right pickle. They had been shut out from borrowing in the financial markets because none of the investors believed they would get their money back. The Greek crisis was triggered by the worldwide recession that had come about due to the GFC. Greece went in to the biggest recession in the world to date even beating the infamous Great Depression of the 1930's in the USA. Unemployment sky rocketed, income fell off a cliff and the country went in to a small scale humanitarian crisis. They even defaulted on a $1.7 billion loan from the International Monetary Fund (IMF). Basically they told the IMF "sorry chaps, we don't have any money to pay you back the money you lent us!"

Other countries had to step in and give Greece money in order to stop the crisis getting even worse! Anyway, you get the picture! A lot of money globally was printed to stop everybody going bankrupt.

After this crisis, the blame game started. The politicians blamed the banks for lending too much money to people who clearly did not have the means to pay it back. The politicians were very quick to forget that they were the ones encouraging everybody to borrow and not bothering to regulate the market.

Back in those days, if I met somebody new, I'd automatically dread them asking what I did for a living. Working in the finance sector was frowned upon during this time, and we were all blamed for the crisis, even though the majority of us had done nothing wrong. It was the usual paint brush approach of politicians to blame anybody in the finance world to save face and score votes with the population.

When I first went to live in Dubai in 2010, Alison and I were invited out one night with a group of friends to go and see some stand-up comedy. When the second act came on the comedian started asking people in the audience what they did for a living and then proceeded to take the piss out of them. We were sat in the front row. OMG! When he asked me what job I did I said: "Binman".

Quite clearly, I was not a binman in Dubai and thankfully he then proceeded to rip me to pieces about trying to convince him I had left the UK to pursue a career as a binman in Dubai. This was fine by me. I took this verbal onslaught from the sharp-witted comedian in good spirits, because I knew I was getting away lightly. Imagine if he had found out I was a banker!

The upshot of the crisis was that regulation entered the financial markets like a bull running through the crowd at a football stadium. There were bodies everywhere! It was, as the saying goes, the equivalent of:

"Shutting the stable door after the horse has bolted."

All of a sudden anybody who worked in finance became scared of their own shadow. The overzealous regulators had paralysed the system. We had gone from zero regulation to heavily regulated virtually overnight. It was a massive overkill. If unregulated is zero and over-regulated is ten, the finance system needs to be somewhere around five or six. It will get there eventually I think, but, going from zero to ten so quickly killed the financial markets.

The effect of this excessive regulation literally shut down the business banks were historically involved in. It was an extraordinary time. Nobody wanted to make a decision on anything in case they were deemed responsible if something went wrong. One mistake in that over-regulated market could see you lose your job, if not your career. Consequently, nothing was done.

People weren't willing to make simple decisions and so the decision would be passed up to their managers. The managers did not want to make the decision in case something went wrong and it was passed further up the chain to senior managers and so on and so on. Nothing was accomplished out of fear and blame!

When a trader in the market has no position and does not want one they say the trader is sitting on their hands. That was exactly what happened to the entire market. Everybody sat on their hands and did nothing. People started becoming wary of the person they sat next to. They stopped talking to each other for fear of incriminating themselves in something they did not even know about and the blame game and paranoia started moving on to the trading floors. People started blaming each other if they made a mistake. It was survival of the fittest, natural selection and blaming others in order to protect yourself was the best defence!

The financial world was a mess. Yes, the banks had made mistakes lending to people who did not have the means to pay it back. The politicians had made mistakes encouraging everybody to own their own house and not regulating the banks. The population had made mistakes borrowing money they could never afford to repay. The bottom line was they all blamed each other rather than taking a long hard look in the mirror and acknowledging their part in the biggest financial mistake of the last 100 years or so. Nobody wanted to see their status and reputation in tatters. It was easier to blame the next guy!

Even now, to this day that blame culture still exists in the financial world and is buried deep within big corporate business. It destroys trust, creativity, energy, morals, ethics and productivity. In short, it ruins a company.

Do not let the blame culture infect the company of YOU. If you make a mistake, take ownership of it. Learn from your mistakes. Yes, it's very easy to blame somebody else if something goes wrong but deep down, if you know you are at fault, act on it.

When you find yourself in a management position or leading a team of staff, lead by example and avoid blamestorming. You can influence the team culture by making it okay to take ownership of mistakes and refusing to make it all about blame.

Everybody makes mistakes. You bring me the perfect person and I will show you a liar. 'Sorry' is not a dirty word. 'Sorry' in my book commands more respect than some lame arse excuse blaming somebody else. 'Sorry' takes ownership of a mistake and, for me, that takes courage. Blaming somebody else for your shortcomings is not going to improve the situation. Only you can improve YOU.

We have all been there, trying to make excuses, blaming somebody or something. A few years ago, I did exactly that to a very good friend of mine who also happened to be my boss, because I did not want to disappoint him.

Around the time I was given the whole continent of Africa to manage, I took my boss down to our office in Johannesburg, South Africa, to see the team we had down there.

The first evening as we relaxed in the bar of our hotel, my boss told me how I needed to make more money for the bank. Choking on my beer, I took this as a rather solid kick in the stomach. Hang on a minute, I had just cleaned up in Nigeria and had produced record revenues for the Middle East and Africa business. He said that now I had South Africa to trade I should be generating even more success. I should be challenging the success of our two biggest business areas, Russia and Turkey!

I proceeded to tell him (in rather strong terms) that he was off his nut! That he was not being fair to me or my team. South Africa was a big market, but it was also a very challenging one. It did not have the regular revenue streams that Russia and Turkey had. I then went on to tell him (again in rather firm terms) that all he ever did was give me the crap jobs, and if he had given me Russia I would be making as much money if not more than the people he had running it.

Basically, I had a large go at the blame game. Rather than taking his comments as a compliment (we had just cracked Nigeria and made a staggering amount of money out of it), and asking him to help me in South Africa, I went on a rant about how other people got it so easy and I got it so hard. I was blaming everybody for something I had not even attempted achieving yet.

My boss went to bed pissed off at me and did not speak to me for the whole of the next day. Eventually I went to him with my tail between my legs and apologised. I admitted that I reacted the way I did because I was scared of disappointing him. We had grown up in the bank together and he was like a brother to me. I later realized there was no need for me to fear disappointing him. He could never be disappointed in me. He always had my back and only ever tried to help me. By indulging in my rant, I had just thrown that friendship back in his face.

To be fair, if he had worded his original statement along the lines of:

"Well done so far in the Middle East and Africa. Now you have South Africa as well we need to get some similar results here!"

I probably would not have told him to piss off as many times as I did. For the record, he left me the bar bill as well. Sneaky!

I apologized for my poor reaction and took ownership of my mistake and fortunately for me everything was fine. If I had lost my cool with someone else in that way, who knows what damage I may have done to my career? Even though it ended well, that event still echoes with me now. Take ownership for your own short comings and better still, don't make them in the first place if you can help it!

Don't blame others for stuff that you control. It will only eat you up and you have to live with it. The more you blame other people the worse you feel. It's ok to make mistakes. How you own those mistakes and learn from them is far more important than running around blaming others. If you know you are wrong, admit it and move on. The longer you leave a problem, the longer and harder it will take to work it out.

CHAPTER 21 - BE KIND

There is a wise old saying in the acting world:

"Be kind to the people you meet on the way up, because you may meet them on the way down."

Life is going to be a lot of ups and downs. You will scale great mountains in life, reaching the summits and attaining your goals. You will also descend to the depths of the valley floor when things don't quite go right for you. On your way up the mountain you will meet many people. Some will be on their way up the mountain and others will be on their way down to the valley floor. Be kind to whoever you meet on your journey because you may meet them again and your circumstances might be reversed.

I recently had a bit of work on a big Disney film at Shepperton studios and my job was to stand-in for the main actor. The job of a stand-in is to be present on set when the director is setting up the scene.

Each scene in a film takes a long time to set up. Lighting has to be perfect, camera angles need to be precise and the microphones need to be positioned to capture the dialogue but not be in the shot. This can - and often does - take a long time. The main actor can't afford to be standing around for hours getting tired while waiting for the crew to get the scene set-up correctly. Instead, the main actor can be relaxing in their trailer, going over lines and preparing for the scene while the stand-in performs this role.

The reason I got the job was down to the fact I looked a little bit like the main actor. I was the same height and build and we both were a little challenged in the hair department: basically, neither of us had much! To the director this is great. When he is setting up the camera angles he gets the same sized actor in the shot. He knows how far his camera can zoom in or pan out given the size of the actor and the set. Due to my comparably sized and follicly challenged head, the director can see where best to place the lighting to eradicate any potential glare.

When the scene is correctly set to the director's liking, the stand-in steps out and the main actor comes in and shoots the scene. The stand-in is clearly not the glamorous side of the acting world! You don't get to walk the red carpet when the premier takes place but it's somewhere to start in the acting world. I gained a lot of experience from being on the set, interacting with the other actors and crew as well as seeing how a big budget feature film is made.

The set of a big Disney film production is packed with people at all different stages of their careers. Actors, directors, sound engineers, lighting engineers, camera crew, safety crew, runners and stand-ins; to mention but a few. Everybody has a job to do. Some are glamorous jobs and some involve some serious grunt work.

Not that I have had the pleasure of working with Tom Hanks (yet!) but I have heard that he is one of the kindest actors in the industry. Always has time for everybody no matter how junior or senior they are in the production. Now there is a guy that has not done too badly for himself and he certainly didn't get to where he is by being arrogant, rude or an arsehole!

I made it my mission that day to meet and shake hands (remember this is prior to COVID-19) with everybody I came in to contact with from the director all the way down to the runners. The runners of today could be the big film directors in 10 years' time. I may get to work with some of these people again and I want them to have only positive memories of me. If

I walk in there and behave like a complete arsehole to everybody, that could be it, my acting prospects might never progress. Even if I'm spotted being arrogant and rude to somebody offset, it could be enough for someone to form a negative impression of me that ends any chance of further potential.

Nobody wants to work with people like that in any field. We all enjoy working with positive, friendly, courteous and polite people, no matter the circumstances. Remember, first impressions count and they're often very difficult to change. All of the things we have in our zero talent and money list will be noticed.

Years from now I may apply for a role in a movie or TV show and the casting director may choose to shortlist me based on my audition. If my picture then gets in front of the producer or the director of the project and they remember me as only being a complete idiot when I was but a lowly stand-in then they may not want to work with me, no matter how good I was in the audition. They will choose somebody else from the shortlist and I will never know that I lost that job because I was an arsehole 10 years ago!

On the other hand, if they remember me being kind, nice, reliable, courteous, hard-working, on time and energetic when they vaguely met me 10 years earlier, then I may get the job ahead of somebody who was a better actor in the audition than me. Again, I may never know that I got the job based on my behaviour as a stand-in 10 years ago.

What you do, how you behave and how you treat others today can have consequences tomorrow. Being kind costs you nothing and is one of the greatest investments you can make in YOU. You may never know the value that investment has given YOU. It's a free option that costs YOU nothing but when exercised freely and often, will have a great influence on your future.

As I grew more senior in the bank, one of my jobs was to look at promotions each year. Managers would put forward their nominations for promotions and we would have a meeting to discuss who we thought should be promoted. Did they deserve to be promoted? Had they been doing the job long enough to have the relevant experience to receive a promotion?

I have always said that the best person for the job should get it irrespective of gender, religion, or race. People should be rewarded on merit. I have never been one for ticking the diversity box just because we have to be seen to be doing it. I have always believed in promoting and rewarding based on effort, experience, performance and suitability.

I actually take the opinion that promoting or rewarding somebody just to tick the diversity box is actually doing that person a disservice. An employee rarely wants to be promoted or rewarded based purely on their gender, religion or race. Nobody wants to have that stigma hanging over them. Nobody wants to hear: "they were only promoted because…" behind their backs. People want to be recognised based on merit and know that they truly earned their promotion fair and square.

Remember Nadine? When we hired Nadine, people were over the moon that we had employed the first female graduate from a Middle Eastern University. I did not want Nadine thinking we had only hired her because somebody insisted we tick the 'political correctness' box. Nadine had not studied hard all her life to be hired because she was female and born in Egypt. Nadine was hired because she was the best fit for our team. Tagging her with the PC banner was bang out of order in my book and I made sure people knew it.

When it came around to promotion and bonus time, my decisions were based on how people performed. Were they team players? Were they good at their job? My decisions weren't based on a single moment in time or their work on one particular project. Instead, I reviewed each employee's performance based on the previous year's work at the bank. Did they treat everybody - no matter their status - with respect? Did they meet their deliverables? Did they help out their colleagues? Did they use their initiative? Did they take ownership of any mistakes they made? Could I rely on them? Were they ready for additional responsibility? All of these factors – and more - would influence my decision-making process.

I remember watching the Chairman of a bank once standing up in front of all the shareholders and employees and declaring the following:

"You will all be pleased to know that we have promoted our first female to the board. This is a milestone for the bank and shows how we embrace diversity."

Something wasn't right in that statement for me. There is nothing wrong in hiring the first female to the board, but announcing it like that! If I was the female employee just hired to the board, I'd be mortified and embarrassed. I would be asking myself if I got the job based on merit or if I was a diversity hire to impress the shareholders. I have no idea if the woman in question had any of those thoughts - as I would have done in her shoes - but that statement did not sit well with me.

If you are doing the right thing people will notice and pay attention. There is no need to announce to the world how diverse you are.

I did have the 'pleasure' of working with one complete arsehole who had no respect for anybody. When I say working with I don't mean literally, thank goodness. He was on a different desk, but our paths would cross from time to time. He believed he was superior to everybody and would not hesitate to screw anybody over to get what he wanted. He would have sold his own grandmother if there was a market for it. He really was a prick and everybody was saying just that behind his back. He treated people with zero respect. However, he made good money for the bank so people seemed to turn a blind eye to his behaviour.

A few years down the line, the financial landscape in the market changed. Some of his deals started going bad, losing money and putting the bank's reputation at risk. When it comes to making money or preserving reputation, the bank will always go for reputation. Reputation is what YOU survive on. Reputation is what YOU need most. Bad reputations = less clients = less business = less profitability and in some cases, bankruptcy.

Remember that well. A long-term positive reputation is one of the most precious assets you can have in any business. Making a short-term profit at the expense of your reputation will destroy your business in the long run.

As his deals went bad, staff were reluctant to help due to the manner in which he had treated them in the past. Nobody wanted to work with him. Nobody wanted to be associated with him and as the pressure grew, rather than trying to mend his relationships and get help, he just continued to blame everybody else. On the way up he behaved badly so on the way down nobody wanted to help. He was subsequently moved on to a different department that was somewhat less glamorous and I wasn't sorry to see him go. What goes around comes around!

"Be kind to people on the way up, because you will meet them on the way down."

IMPACT STATEMENT: LINUS

Linus was due to sit his final A Level exams in Art and Design Technology.

"My first reaction to hearing the news was happy. I thought, great! No exams! But later on, I started to feel like I was missing out on something. I was setting out to try and beat my predicted grades and was almost looking forward to the exams.

It was only until later on I also heard schools were closing on Friday. This is what made me very sad. Going through almost the two years of work with friends you see every day suddenly end, was hard to believe. I think once you've had time to think about it you start to realise how important school is, not just for learning but to be with friends and enjoying yourself.

I don't think not taking your exams will affect your future as they're just exams. You can retake them later on if you really want to. Your future depends on you and anything is possible if you want it bad enough. But I also feel our year may think we never completed it or missed out on grades that showed our hard work rather than grades predicted. I do feel our year have left the school unfinished, because we have.

However, for me I don't think it worries me too much about moving as my interests are art which is portfolio based. For other people taking academic subjects I think it might hinder them in the future.

Although not completing our exams, I do feel a celebration is definitely needed. It may not be the same feeling for everyone without their exam grades, but more of a celebration of the years you've worked together and the friends made."

CHAPTER 22 - DEAL WITH IT

Before I go any further I would just like to thank all of my impact statement contributors. To Amy, Billie, Charlie, Max, Annalise, Cormac, Alice, Katia and Linus, I thank you for allowing me to share your thoughts and words in this book. I hope you will all go on to achieve great things and will not let this situation hold you back. I have the greatest of confidence in each of you and wish you all the best for the future. Please keep in touch and let me know how you're getting on. In fact it would be a very good sequel to this book. "Where are they now?"

In reading all of the impact statements, I've come to identify a unifying initial response of relief. Happy days, exams are cancelled. No revising, no sleepless nights, no pressure. We can also see that some young people not in this situation are thinking what a lucky bunch this lot are! Why couldn't this have happened next year when I have my final exams?

But then you read on and the emotions soon change to sadness, anxiety and the fear of never knowing:

Could we have done better?

The presence of "never knowing" takes its toll on mental wellbeing.

While this is certainly an unprecedented and extreme event that nobody could have predicted, it does serve to show us the value of each of the topics we have talked about: being on time, work ethic, effort, body language, energy, attitude, passion, listening, doing extra, preparation, cutting out pointless stuff, taking ownership and being kind.

You can go back to every chapter where we have discussed "things that require zero talent" and write your own chapter using COVID-19 as your example.

Remember earlier in the book I said:

If I had made an announcement to every student back in September 2019, who was due to take final exams in Summer 2020 that said:

"In January 2020 a virus is going to come out of China which will spread across the globe in a pandemic that will kill many people and infect a great many more. The world will go in to lockdown…..Oh and by the way your final exams will be cancelled and you will be given a grade that reflects how much effort you have put in to the course, your attitude to learning and your teachers, not to mention how well you do in the mock exams. Just saying!"

Would you have believed me?

The unpredictability of this event shows us that while we need to live life demonstrating all of those values we need to be doing it every day because we just don't know what's going to happen tomorrow. Live in the present. Yes, you have goals, dreams and aspirations but live within the limits of what you can control in the present, and day by day you will get one step closer to your dream.

We have no idea what is around life's next bend but if you have the basics covered you can be ready for it.

But let's not dwell on what has happened. You can't dwell on:

"if only this had not happened"

or

"I wonder what direction my life would have taken if I had sat the exams."

You cannot answer that question so why dwell on it? You can have a guess but that is all it would be, an educated guess. Something that can never be proven.

Young people, you have this situation and WE have to deal with it. Whether you were due to sit exams this year or not, a chapter in your life has been interrupted. You have to own it. Don't dwell in the blame game. Don't let COVID-19 define you. When something does not turn out the way you expected in the future, don't blame COVID-19. What is done is done. We can't rewind COVID-19. We can't erase it and re-record. How you deal with it will define you greatly as you move forward. Are you going to live forever under the COVID-19 cloud or are you going to punch it in the face and move on?

As Linus wrote:

"Your future depends on you and anything is possible if you want it bad enough."

Life is a journey and this is just one of life's stations that you are passing through. Remember, you will scale many great peaks and descend to many valley floors on your journey. Some elements of society will feel pity for the way in which the pandemic interrupted your education; others less generous will hold it against you because your experience was different to theirs. There's nothing you can do about how this course of events will be viewed by others. The only thing within your control is how you react to the situation.

If you are still bothered by the qualifications that were 'given' to you then you can choose to sit your exams at a later date if you feel so inclined. But don't do it for society. Only do it if you feel you need to lay any residual demons to rest. Do it for your own peace of mind. Do it for you!

If you are ready to move forward to your next challenge use this entire experience in a positive way to get up and go again. Go and prove to society that you will not be judged by this situation, that this will not hold you back.

Remember Nelson Mandela once said:

"Do not judge me by my successes, judge me by how many times I fell down and got back up again."

The next great peak is waiting for you. Go and plant your flag in it!

CHAPTER 23 - BE TRUE TO YOURSELF

YOU have the ability to do everything on that list. YOU have those tools at your disposal, and they are free. They don't cost YOU anything. They are tools that the company of YOU have in abundance.

Apply them correctly and you will see so many good things come your way. Be true to what you believe in and your dreams. Don't try and be something you are not.

Be yourself and don't let anything or anyone hold you back. Don't try to be somebody you think other people want you to be. You have to be yourself. It's a little bit like acting. I can be given a character to play and I will go away and do my research on that character. I will practice that character and take on the mannerisms of that character. Dress me as that character and you won't know it's me up to a point. But I can't do that 24/7 for the rest of my life. I will eventually revert to being me again. That character is not me. That character does not have my DNA. I can give you a good performance of that character but truthfully, I can only maintain it for so long before my true self shines through. I can't fool you forever. You will work me out and realise that the character I am playing is not the real me.

It's the same in life. You can't be something you're not. People who try are often identified as being two-faced, fakes and phonies. I'm sure you've met a few and you know what I mean. You are who you are and you must be true to yourself. People want to see the real person, not a projection.

If something isn't right, you have to change it.

I will leave you with an early episode from my life. I had to make a change and it took a lot of courage, but it allowed me to grow and be the person I was.

I was brought up in a very religious family. My mum and dad were Christians. I was taken to church twice on Sundays from the age of zero to 16. We were not allowed to watch the television on a Sunday. I was not allowed to play for my local football team because they played matches on a Sunday. No work was ever done on a Sunday and certainly no shopping like we have today. Back then very few - if any - shops even opened on a Sunday.

In my early years, I thought this was normal. I was born into a religious family and therefore I was brought up in the ways my parents believed were right. I did not know any different. This was fine, up until a point.

As a kid, I went to Sunday school and the youth club that was part of the church, but by about 14 years old, like many teenagers I started to develop my own thoughts on the topic. Church life wasn't for me and I started to resent it a bit. I did not like going to school on Monday morning and listening to all my mates talking about the football match they had played on Sunday. I felt left out and uncomfortably different.

I carried on going to church because I did not want to disappoint my parents. I was trying to be somebody I was not because that's what I thought my parents wanted me to be. I had grown and developed my own feelings and thoughts on the topic of life and religion, but I was not expressing them. Instead, I was actually suppressing them because I did not want to disappoint my family. In truth, I was living a lie. I was pretending to be the person I believed everybody else wanted to see.

I had no interest in the church services and didn't enjoy listening to something I really did not believe in. I learnt to play the guitar just so I could play music for the little kids to sing to at Sunday School. Once my music job was done I either sat around and entertained the younger kids or snuck out the side door and went for a walk. Either way, I was not sat on a hard, wooden bench listening to something that did not interest me. That was the morning service sorted. The evening service was a bit trickier. There was no Sunday School and no little kids to play guitar for. I had to lump it and play noughts and crosses with another bored friend who was sitting next to me!

For a couple of years, I endured this routine and kept quiet about how I felt and what I was thinking. I did not want to upset my mum and dad.

In those two years, I contemplated how I was eventually going to break away from church and religion. How was I going to get out of this without disappointing my parents and bringing shame on the family? My parents' friends in the church didn't seem to have this issue with their kids. (I later found out a few of them did!) What would people say? I silently wrestled with this problem for two years and felt trapped.

When I turned 16, I finally plucked up the courage to tell my mum and dad that church was not for me and I did not want to go anymore. I was telling them truthfully that they were holding me back. I could not keep up this church-going character any longer. I had to live my life and be me.

Having dropped this bombshell, I nervously waited for them to explode. Surprisingly, the explosion never came. My mum was naturally upset. She wanted what she thought was best for me and in her eyes church and religion was best for me. My sister, who is five years older than me had accepted religion and God. It had been expected that I would do the same.

My dad, who I thought would absolutely flip and be most disappointed in me, just looked at me and said:

"It's fine son. You have to live your life the way you think is best. I hope one day you will come back to religion but it's not my place to force it on you. I respect you for telling me and I will support you in everything you do and don't worry about mum, she will understand in time."

In that moment two of the most wonderful things happened to me.

Firstly, my relationship with my dad changed. As a kid growing up I had been much more of a mummy's boy, but that day my dad and I became rock solid. We became best friends. There was always one thing that you could say about my dad. If he told you something, he meant it and you would never, ever have to doubt it – and I never had cause to doubt it. When I said, I didn't want to go to University and wanted to go into the city, my dad backed me one hundred per cent. When things weren't going well for me in the city and rejections were coming thick and fast, he picked me up and instilled in me the belief that I would succeed. He was a great man and I miss him.

Secondly, I was liberated from the considerable burden I had been carrying around for two years. It was the burden of feeling boxed in and trapped by something I had no interest in. I had been living a lie and was not able to go forward. From the day of my liberation I was able to develop me, the product. I could be the person I felt I was destined to be.

Since my liberation, I always tell people that I was the odd ball of the family in a half joking sort of way, to make light of it.

"I was the rebel that rebelled."

In fact, I wasn't rebelling, I was growing. Rather than being a sheep that followed, I became a shepherd and led. I had finally freed myself to forge my own path rather than have someone tell me how I should live my life.

I should say here that I don't have a problem with faith or religion or any people for whom religion is a way of life. That is a matter for them and I am completely supportive. It just wasn't for me or rather isn't for me at this time. Perhaps, like my dad said, I may come back to it at some stage but right now I am focusing on living life the way I feel I should live it. Do what you feel is right and best for you.

Where I have a problem is watching people who clearly are doing something that does not make them happy just so they don't upset some form of balance equation. The balance could be family, friends or colleagues. Essentially, they are being held back in pursuing their dreams because they are afraid to stand up or lack the courage to make a change for what they believe in.

All through my teenage years my dad had serious health problems and he cheated death nine times. Every time the doctors told us they were not optimistic about his chances, he would bounce back and prove them wrong. He lived long enough to see me marry Alison. He lived long enough to see both Charlie and Alex, but eventually he ran out of time.

My dad died in 2012 and I was living in Dubai at the time. My mum called and told me the doctors did not rate his chances of pulling through very highly this time around, which given his previous track record I took with a grain of salt. But this time my mum sounded different. She knew this was going to be his final bow to the audience of life so I jumped on a plane and flew home to see him.

When I arrived, my dad was in immense pain. The doctors were effectively keeping him alive but I knew that was not what my dad would want. We all agreed they should stop the medication for the infections that were attacking him, make him comfortable and let nature take its course.

The night before I flew back to Dubai I sat with my dad at his bedside and read him the Lord's Prayer. He knew he was dying, and he was comfortable with it. His faith enabled him to embrace it. I struggled to get to the end of the prayer and the tears were streaming down my face. I couldn't believe I was losing the man I most respected in my life. At the end of the prayer my dad looked at me with eyes only I could interpret. He was immensely proud of me and all I had achieved. And then he waved me to go. He was a great man and I miss him dearly.

If something or someone in your life is holding you back don't be afraid to change it. You might just be surprised at the response you get. It's your life and you have to live it to the full. If that means telling loved ones something isn't right for you, go ahead and tell them. Trust me, you'll feel much better for it and will be free to commence your new path.

Success in life comes with doing something you truly believe in, something you are passionate about that makes you genuinely happy. Success can't be measured in money and if you're doing something purely to appease others, you'll never achieve true happiness. If you believe in what you do and it makes you happy, all the other things will fall naturally into place. If people truly love you and want the best for you, they will understand. It may hurt them initially, but they will have more respect for you in the long run.

Your life is yours and yours alone. Don't let anything or anybody hold you back or distract you from achieving your dreams. If you have the power to change something in your life for the better, do it. Never give yourself the chance to regret.

I like to think life is like a game of golf. When you play golf, you can surround yourself with people who can give you lessons. People who can suggest what shot you should play, what direction to hit the ball in, what club to use, but ultimately only you can take the shot. The choice of how you play the game and ultimately win or lose is down to you. But remember, you only get one game of life. You can't repeat it. You can't rewind and re-record.

It's your life and it's your choice. You have many people and resources who can help you make those choices but only you can dictate your own destiny. Choose wisely. Listen and learn so you can make informed decisions but make the choice that you think is best for you. You may make a wrong choice here and there, but embrace the consequences and try again. Never give up. You will make the correct choice in the end.

I can't change you. Your friends and family might try, but they can't really change you either. They can only help you and guide you, but they can't change you. If you want to change you have to make that choice for yourself and I hope I've provided some inspiration on a number of ways in which you can do this.

Never more has the world needed our young people. You are not forgotten about. You are all very important and crucial to dragging us out of this COVID mess.

Your world needs YOU!

Life is a journey and the future is just as uncertain now as it has ever been. But out of uncertainty comes opportunity. You have the opportunity. How you embrace the uncertainty is what will define you. COVID-19 is just a small hump in the road that lies ahead of you and in time will start to appear behind you.

Life is not a destination that you have to get to as quickly as possible. We are all on that journey. The secret to a wonderful journey is to make sure you are in the driving seat! So put your foot down, get over this hump and carry on down the road. Remember, there is a place in the world for everybody. Find your place and do great things. Your life is ready for you to grab it and own it, to do great things and achieve your dreams.

Let's punch COVID-19 in the gut and move on. We have so much to achieve and so little time to do it. Let's get started.

Nobody cares more for your life than you do, so start caring how you live and start living like you care!

And let me know how you're getting on.

AFTERWORD

To be honest, I never set out to write a book.

One day I was having a coffee with a good friend of mine, Dave Vaughn from the Smart Collaborative. Dave does a lot of work with young people and whenever we are together at some stage we will talk about young people and the challenges they face today.

Over coffee I was telling Dave how the pressure our young people are under today is immense and that in my opinion, the rise in mental health issues in our young people today are directly linked to that pressure. I made the point that that pressure could be managed with just a few simple life hacks and tips that I had learned in the banking world. Dave asked if I could put a presentation together that we could take in to schools and talk to students about.

So I started to write some things down, but once I started I really could not stop. Hence we have a book.

Thanks Dave for starting me on this journey!

ACKNOWLEDGEMENTS

I would never have come this far without the support and input from my wife Alison, my son Charlie and my daughter Alex. Our conversations around the dinner table on many of the topics I have covered in the book were insightful, funny, intriguing and revealing. Contrary to what you might think, being a parent or guardian isn't easy. You don't come with an instruction manual when you're born, so spare a thought for your parents and guardians. We are all trying to do our best for you, but it's a learning curve for us too! Remember, we never stop learning. I am immensely proud of both Charlie and Alex. They make life interesting and fun and I look forward to seeing what they get up to in the years ahead.

I have to say a big thank you to my Mum and Dad as well. Without them, well none of this would have been possible as we discussed back in Chapter 5.

My journey through the financial world enabled me to meet and work with some wonderful people across the globe I will never forget and I thank you all for knowing me. Some of those people are mentioned in this book and I want to say a special thank you to everyone who agreed to let me include them in my anecdotes.

To Chris, Emily, Nadine, Ali, Shoaib, Jamie, Bud and Lisa, I thank you.

To Richard Robinson, not a day goes by when I don't think about you chief. You were my greatest ever employee, but more importantly you were a terrific friend and colleague. Our bond made work fun and enjoyable, and together we achieved great success. You changed my life and I will forever be grateful. One day we will work together again. I will never forget you.

To Charlotte Robinson, Richard's wife I would like to say thank you for letting me talk about your husband. Richard will always be with you and the children.

A very big thank you goes out to my Impact Statement contributors. Amy, Billie, Charlie, Max, Annalise, Cormac, Alice, Katia and Linus. Thank you for agreeing to help me with your thoughts and emotions. Thank you for being honest, open and raw with your contributions and I wish you all the best for the future. I will be watching with interest to see where your journey takes you. I know you will all do great things. Just make sure you are happy!

To my former employers, I thank you for taking the time to read my book and allowing me to write about my time with the bank. It was a great place to work. A corporation that really looked after its employees and treated them like family.

To everybody that knows me or I have had the pleasure of meeting through my journey, you have all played a part in shaping me, in developing me in to the person I am today and I thank you all from the bottom of my heart because you have made me happy.

To the readers, I thank you for taking the time to read my book. I hope I have been helpful in some way. If you want to let me know how you're getting on, share your success stories or have an Impact Statement you'd like to share, send it to me at simonwalterauthor@gmail.com

Just remember, be YOU and be happy.

ADDITIONAL RESOURCES

I have taken the liberty of putting together a couple of additional resources for you to access that may help you on your journey.

Who Moved My Cheese by Dr Spencer Johnson is a book I read when I left a 25 year career in the financial world behind me.

Next, I would like to point you in the direction of YouTube and a speech that was made by Admiral William H McRaven in 2014.

Admiral McRaven is a highly decorated Navy veteran with more than 37 years of service and I believe this inspiring speech should be on the curriculum in every educational institution across the world.

The speech is called University of Texas at Austin 2014 Commencement Address – Admiral William H McRaven.

You can also find his book Make Your Bed by William H. McRaven on Amazon.

Earlier in the book we talked about how good it is to talk. To tell somebody how you feel. Sometimes it's not easy to talk to family, friends, teachers etc. Sometimes it's easier to talk to somebody you don't know.

Child Helpline International brings many of the helplines around the world together in one directory. They cover 139 countries around the world, showing you what is available in where you live. They also have some great articles and blogs on the website and you can visit them at www.childhelplineinternational.org

Lastly, if you would like to leave me some comments, feedback, an impact statement or let me know how you're getting on then please contact me at simonwalterauthor@gmail.com

Good luck on your journey!

Printed in Poland
by Amazon Fulfillment
Poland Sp. z o.o., Wrocław

65758991R00087